D1600512

TWISTED
CONFESSIONS

TWISTED CONFESSIONS

The True Story Behind the Kitty Genovese and
Barbara Kralik Murder Trials

Charles E. Skoller

Twisted Confessions: The True Story Behind the Kitty Genovese and Barbara Kralik Murder Trials
Published by Bridgeway Books
P.O. Box 80107
Austin, Texas 78758

For more information about our books, please write to us, call 512.478.2028, or visit our website at www.bridgewaybooks.net.

Library of Congress Control Number: 2007939649

ISBN-13: 978-1-934454-17-6
ISBN-10: 1-934454-17-6

All of the names of the individuals mentioned and/or described in the book are factual. However, any quoted conversations the author or others had with named individuals, some of which are verbatim and some of which are the substance of the conversations, are based on the author's recollections of the same, newspaper articles, actual interviews with the person involved, trial transcripts and other research.

10 9 8 7 6 5 4 3 2 1

To Myrna, my partner in love and life.

In Memory of
       Kitty, Barbara, and Annie Mae

Justice is truth in action.
—Benjamin Disraeli

ACKNOWLEDGMENTS

As I started writing this book and my thoughts and memories began to concentrate on the events described herein that turned out to be the most exhilarating period of my professional life as an attorney, I came to realize my true intention. Having reached the twilight of my life, I asked myself what legacy I could best leave to my grandchildren and their future generations. The legacy turned out to be twofold. First and foremost is to offer the advice that a worthwhile goal can be set in one's life and achieved, no matter how difficult it is or how long it takes to accomplish the goal. Secondly, while I believe my grandchildren know I love them dearly and I feel their love as well, they do not know of my early life beyond this relationship.

It is my deepest hope that these legacies will some day and in some way benefit Brian, Ravit, Niev, Robert, Corey, Jennifer, Shiran, Sydney, Max, Joshua, Sara, Shani and those grandchildren I have yet to meet.

Grampa Charlie
Thanksgiving Day, November 22, 2007

PROLOGUE

It was a warm day in April 1964 when I was handed a note directing me to report to Frank O'Connor, District Attorney of the borough of Queens, as soon as the trial I was prosecuting recessed for the day. I glanced at the handwritten note and set it aside. The Chief, as O'Connor was known to his staff, didn't mention why he had summoned me. The jury in the kidnapping, rape, and robbery trial I had prosecuted was about to announce its verdict, and I assumed he simply wanted a personal briefing. This would be the first time I reported a verdict directly to the Chief. Normally, his Supreme Court Trial Bureau chief, Frank Cacciatore, reported verdicts. Other than that, there seemed nothing exceptional about the summons. Little did I know that I was about to set out on the most exhausting, disturbing, and exhilarating journey of my professional career.

I was an assistant District Attorney assigned to the Supreme Court Trial Bureau of the Queens District Attorney's Office. I was young, ambitious, and completely committed to what I saw as one of our country's highest ideals: the pursuit of justice. The trial winding down represented just the sort of case that fueled my pursuit. The girl who had been brutally kidnapped and raped was a mere fifteen years old, and as if that ordeal weren't bad enough, she'd endured the grueling experience of a mistrial. I had tried this case once before, and it ended in a hung jury.

1

The jurors came down eleven to one for conviction. The lone holdout, the other jurors reported to the trial judge, Albert Bosch, claimed that he could never, under any circumstances, convict a person of a crime. That hung jury—the first I experienced as a prosecutor—proved to be an invaluable lesson in the days and months to come.

As I waited in Judge Bosch's wood-paneled courtroom for the verdict in the retrial, my main concern was the specter of a second hung jury. The evidence was overwhelming against the defendant. He had been apprehended in the middle of the night, fleeing the scene with the victim's wallet and wristwatch. He had been quickly and easily picked out of a police lineup by the victim, and he readily confessed to the crime. But overwhelming evidence didn't always result in justice.

It was about 4:00 p.m. when Judge Bosch announced that the jury had reached its verdict. Shortly thereafter, the jurors filed into the courtroom, and the foreman stood up to read the verdict: guilty on all counts. My relief was tempered by an almost painful grimace on the judge's face. The guilty man would be sentenced to life in prison, and Judge Bosch had no discretion in the sentencing. Whatever Bosch's regrets, I felt no sympathy whatsoever for the defendant, knowing the injury and emotional trauma he had inflicted on the teenager that I thought of as my client. For me, prosecuting cases like this was always a personal affair.

After Judge Bosch discharged the jurors, I hurried out of the courtroom to report to the Chief. My post trial practice was to thank jurors for their service and sometimes to discuss the verdict, but when Frank O'Connor summoned one of his assistant DAs, there was no time to waste.

Prior to his election as District Attorney, O'Connor had been a defense attorney and New York state senator. Respected by the defense bar and police alike, and beloved by his staff, O'Connor had earned a solid reputation for impartiality in the prosecution of criminal cases. Perhaps it was the result of his having defended Emanuel Balestrero, the Stork Club musician wrongly identified by a number of eyewitnesses as the perpetrator of an armed robbery—an incident that Alfred Hitchcock made into the movie *The Wrong Man*. In any event, O'Connor had developed a "wrong-man" complex. In the prosecution of any crime where identification was at issue, a confession was questionable, or objective evidence was lacking to support a confession, his paramount concern was that the innocent not be pronounced guilty. All of O'Connor's assistant DAs were duty bound to assure the Chief that there was no doubt as to the guilt of any accused person.

There was also a personal reason Frank O'Connor wanted to maintain the integrity of his office. Arguably the brightest light in the Democratic Party in New York State, he was considered the leading candidate to run against Nelson Rockefeller for governor. Scandal wasn't something he courted.

I headed over to O'Connor's office, wondering how he would greet the news of the verdict. As soon as I made it through the door, I almost did a double take. For there, next to O'Connor's desk, sat Supreme Court Trial Bureau Chief Frank Cacciatore and Investigation and Homicide Bureau Chief Bernard Patten—the heads of the two most important and sensitive bureaus in the Queens District Attorney's Office. What were they doing here? Covering up my surprise, I reported the verdict.

O'Connor usually projected an almost priestly aura of detachment, but now, leaning against his desk with his arms folded, he had a concerned look on his face. "Fine, Charlie," he said, "but that's not the reason I called you here. I'm assigning you to the Kitty Genovese trial with Cacciatore. You'll also be prosecuting Alvin Mitchell for the Barbara Kralik murder, which has been compromised by Kitty's killer's confession to Barbara's murder. As a consequence, we have two confessions to the same crime. The Kralik and Genovese cases are pending before Judge Shapiro."

I was stunned. It didn't seem possible. Kitty Genovese had been viciously stabbed to death in Kew Gardens on March 13, 1964, while her neighbors heard her screams from their apartment windows and looked on passively. No one had intervened or called for help, at least not until it was too late. The outrageous incident had been reported in glaring headlines across the country and cast a shadow over the borough of Queens. Everyone from coast to coast, it seemed, including President

Lyndon Johnson, was weighing in on the failure of Kitty's neighbors to respond to her screams for help. The incident opened up a whole new phenomenon for students of social psychology to explore and puzzle over: the Kitty Genovese syndrome.

The Kralik homicide was slightly less sensational, but it too had been plastered all over New York's papers. On July 20, 1963, Barbara Kralik had been stabbed to death while asleep in her home in Springfield Gardens. The *New York Daily News* had run front-page articles and photographs of Barbara and her family, including one showing the porch window through which it was believed Barbara's killer had entered the home. The universal fear and vulnerability New Yorkers felt was fueled by the circumstances of Barbara's homicide.

Like the victim in the case I had just prosecuted, Barbara was a mere fifteen years old. The girl's life had been suddenly and violently ended while she slept in a peaceful community surrounded by her family. It sent a collective shudder down the community's spine.

Annie Mae Johnson's murder a month before Kitty's had received scant press attention. Her body had been found in her living room, partially burned. The autopsy stated the cause of death as stabbing with an ice pick.

They wanted me, a lawyer admitted to the bar only four years earlier, with just over two years of trial experience, to prosecute these high-profile cases?

O'Connor stood up and began pacing back and forth. "As you probably know," he went on, "we anticipate Cacciatore's appointment to the criminal court bench at any time. It may be before the Genovese trial, so you'll have to prepare the case with Frank in the event you have to try it alone. You'll also investigate and prepare the Kralik homicide—alone—so in case I decide to go ahead with that trial, you'll be prepared. In view of the relationship between the two cases, you'll have to be up to snuff on both." He stopped pacing and faced me. "How familiar are you with them?"

"I've read the newspapers and had some general discussions with others in the office." I told him the little I knew—that there were major problems with the police department's investigation and that our own

DA's investigation into the Kralik homicide was problematic as well. This was due to the fact that two people had confessed separately to the Kralik murder. Genovese's killer was the second person to confess to the Kralik homicide, and there were several reasons to believe his confession was true. Media outlets were demanding a new investigation of the connection between the two homicides.

"We'll meet tomorrow morning at ten to go over each case and decide how best to proceed," O'Connor said.

A little recklessly, I looked O'Connor in the eyes and asked, "Why me?"

"For a number of reasons. Both trials will be before Judge Shapiro, who's told me he feels you're ready for a high-profile homicide case. You seem to have developed a reputation for thorough trial preparation and investigation—they'll both be essential if I decide to proceed in the Kralik homicide. Furthermore, you don't automatically accept the police versions of what occurred, and I have my doubts about them as well. I know you're dogged and never give up in any case you believe in; you proved that in your retrial of the kidnapping case. On top of that, the defense in the Genovese homicide is expected to be insanity, and Cacciatore here tells me you've devoted some time to the study of such a defense—that you'll be able to handle it without too much difficulty."

He handed me the DA and police files for the three cases and sent me home to look them over. During the ride, my head buzzed with anticipation. Prosecuting the Genovese case! It would be a daunting challenge, and I wondered if I was up to the job. Of course you are, I said to myself. Just take it one step at a time.

I lived in a one-family attached house in Flushing with my wife Bernice, two daughters, and a son. This was the first time I had brought files home from the DA's office, and to concentrate on them I would need some privacy, which is hard to come by in a household with children as young as mine. Beth, the oldest, was four, Robert was three, and my youngest, Caren, would be two in November. So after kissing the kids and giving Bernice a quick wrap-up of the trial that had just ended, I retreated to my finished basement, a den and dining room, spread the files across the table, and began trying to reassemble the bits and pieces of two of the most sensational crimes in Queens history. The third related crime, the murder of Annie Mae Johnson, promised to complicate matters. I would soon learn that the three cases were bound to each other in ways that can only be described as a prosecutor's nightmare.

CHAPTER ONE

Queens is the largest borough in New York City. In 1963, the native born still thought of it as the "country suburbs," not yet infected by the urban problems of the three neighboring boroughs—Manhattan, Brooklyn, and the Bronx. But Queens was changing. The farms that had once separated its villages were being replaced by apartment buildings, rapid transit lines, and highways. The residents of one-family homes no longer outnumbered apartment dwellers, with newcomers moving from Brooklyn and the Bronx to escape the blight and crime of those more populated boroughs. Queens was losing the battle to retain its character as a safe and comfortable residential community.

Until the early 1960s, it was homicides in Manhattan, Brooklyn, and the Bronx that monopolized the crime headlines in New York's newspapers and on the broadcast news. Then the tables turned with a string of murders in Queens: Barbara Kralik's in 1963, Kitty Genovese's in 1964, and Annie Mae Johnson's that same year. Almost overnight, it seemed, homicides in Queens had become front-page news not just across New York City but across the nation as well. The lion's share of attention went to the Kitty Genovese case, much to the shame and embarrassment of the citizens of Queens. Ironically, the community of Kew Gardens, where Kitty's neighbors had looked on passively—or with morbid fascination—while she was being hacked to death, housed government offices, including the borough's criminal justice infrastructure. Kew Gardens and, by association, the one-time country suburb of Queens had become synonymous nationwide with impersonal urban crime and shocking moral indifference.

When I went home that night with the DA and police files it was a baptism by fire. Though I possessed the confidence of youth and had considerable success with the cases I had prosecuted, there was little in my background that guaranteed I would succeed in unraveling the truth behind these crimes or in putting the killers behind bars.

The middle of three sons, I was born in 1932 in Brownsville, a lower-middle-class community of mostly Jewish families in Brooklyn. Our neighborhood was secure and crime free. The only disputes were petty disagreements between friends that broke out during games of punch ball and stickball. I can't recall a single crime committed on my street, Lincoln Place, and nothing about the insular world there could have prepared me for what I would eventually face as a prosecutor.

My father, Murray Skoller, was a shoe store manager who helped unionize retail shoe employees in Brooklyn and Queens and eventually became secretary of the union. He had an exceptional work ethic, lived by a strict moral code, and was as devoted to his children as he was to his work and his union. I had the utmost respect for him. My mother, Jean, was a bookkeeper turned homemaker and the unchallenged guardian of her sons' behavior. An excellent cook, she demanded that we boys finish every last morsel on our plates. "The children of Europe are starving, eat," she used to demand.

Our household included a third adult, David Ayman, my mother's brother. Uncle Dave was blessed with an exceptional mind. As a high school teacher who had completed his master's degree in mathematics at nineteen, he devoted countless hours to helping me in my studies. I basked in his light and excelled in school.

As important as my education was to my parents, so too was work ethic, and at the ripe age of twelve I got a job after school with a dental mechanic, delivering prosthetics to dentists and oral surgeons and dutifully turning over all earnings to my mother. At the age of fourteen, as soon as I was able to obtain working papers from the New York State Labor Department, I became a delivery boy for a florist, working three days after school and full days on Saturdays and Sundays.

Toward the end of middle school I took the entrance examination for Stuyvesant High School and was accepted. It was on the Lower East Side of Manhattan, an hour-long commute from home, and I had to learn how to juggle schoolwork and my demanding job with the florist. At the age of sixteen, I graduated from high school and went on to Brooklyn College. By now, the heavy demands of school and work were taking their toll; I couldn't concentrate on either, and I was suffering from the lack of a social life.

It all came to a head in February 1951. I had to get away, and without telling anyone in my family, I enlisted in the U.S. Army. Six months later, following basic training, I landed in Korea and was detached to provide air-ground communication support for the First British Commonwealth Division. This harrowing tour of combat duty was to have a profound effect on my life. I promised myself that if I survived unscathed, I would complete my college education and prepare for a career in the legal profession.

I was discharged in January 1954, following a one-year tour of duty in the Pentagon, and returned to Brooklyn College. I graduated in 1957 with a liberal arts degree, got married, and after a short honeymoon, entered Brooklyn Law School. I threw myself into the study of law, attending summer classes while clerking for a small civil practice firm in Jamaica, Queens. After graduation in 1959, I took the July bar examination, passed, and was admitted the following year to the practice of law in New York State. The law firm I'd been clerking for hired me as an associate attorney, and I began investigating various civil matters and analyzing related legal issues.

Meanwhile, I became active in a reform democratic organization that defeated an old-line, boss-dominated democratic organization in a primary election in Flushing. As a result, in January 1962, Frank O'Connor appointed me to his office as an assistant District Attorney. In those days, all appointments to the District Attorneys' offices in New York State were political ones, and mine was no exception. I was first assigned to the Adolescent Court Bureau, where I conducted preliminary hearings of youthful offenders charged with felonies and misdemeanors in addition to trials of some minor violations. It was my first experience with trial work, and I dove into it with abandon, starved for knowledge and experience.

A few hours before our office's annual Christmas dinner that year, Frank O'Connor sent for me. As soon as I closed the door behind me, he said, "Charlie, we're transferring you to the Supreme Court Trial Bureau under Frank Cacciatore." It was the major trial bureau of the DA's office and handled jury and non-jury trials of all major crimes, including murder.

I was flattered and overjoyed, if somewhat skeptical. Only thirty years old, I had never handled a jury trial, criminal or civil. Apparently several lower-court judges had made the recommendation, and O'Connor had reviewed copies of several preliminary hearings and minor trials I'd prosecuted. "You seem to have an affinity for trial work," he reassured me.

The transfer was welcome recognition for the effort that I had put into my assigned cases. The job of prosecutor, I firmly believed, was an important public duty, and privately I vowed to fulfill my obligation to the best of my ability. Little did I know how severely the job would test me.

The supreme court in Queens had four trial parts. Prosecutors remained in the same part, while trial justices regularly moved from one part to another. Each part had two prosecutors, one on trial and the other preparing cases for trial.

After I'd been assigned to a part, my first trial justice, Anthony M. Livoti, summoned me to his office. He wanted to know how I'd evaluated each of my cases and whether I anticipated a trial or a plea bargain. A former trial prosecutor himself, Justice Livoti offered valuable advice that I have tried to follow ever since, in civil as well as criminal trials. He taught me that laying the groundwork—thoroughly preparing in advance of a trial, gaining a solid command of the facts, gathering detailed information about every possible witness, and anticipating evidentiary and other legal issues that might arise—often tipped the scales, bringing about a successful prosecution.

Determined to follow his advice, I devised a methodical approach to trial work. For every case, I would prepare a complete pretrial outline that listed the following: each count of the indictment; the controlling statutes and other rules of law; and the names, addresses, and pedigrees of witnesses, with a synopsis of what I expected their testimony to be. I included every possible evidentiary issue that might arise, including previous court opinions and decisions related to such issues. I also took up the practice—which among assistant DAs was nonexistent in those days—of preparing requests to the judge in charging the jury, that is, in issuing final instructions to jurors before they commenced their deliberations. Whenever a trial justice asked me if the People were ready for trial, my answer was always a confident yes.

My first jury trials took place in January 1963. The experience was electrifying, and I wanted to be in court every day. Thanks to the detective assigned to assist me with trial preparation, I was able to prepare in the evenings and on weekends and actually be in court during the week. Turning over to other attorneys the civil practice I was permitted to handle outside the DA's office, I devoted all my time and energy to prosecuting trials.

In my first month on the new job, whenever I had a spare moment, I visited Frank Cacciatore's courtroom. He was in the midst of prosecuting a woman and her lover for the murder of her husband, a physician. I studied Cacciatore's demeanor and the way he approached the jurors during jury selection and the actual trial. Frank was my standard for a prosecutor, and I learned a lot from him. His forceful and confident style conveyed to a jury his belief in the merit of the case that he was prosecuting. I learned that a jury could not be convinced if they thought you didn't believe in your own case.

In February 1963, Justice J. Irwin Shapiro, who was considered the most brilliant and respected trial judge in the borough, was assigned to my trial part. One of the youngest people ever to be admitted to the

New York bar, he was a former chief assistant DA of Queens County and had served as counsel to the governor of New York and as a judge in every trial court—civil, criminal, and domestic relations—in Queens. He possessed broad intellectual interests and was a voracious reader, always seeking knowledge ranging far beyond his legal requirements as a judge. His mind moved at a speed that was difficult to keep up with. Not possessed of an abundance of patience, he gave prosecutors and defense attorneys little time to think or space to maneuver. Woe to the prosecutor trying a case before Judge Shapiro in which the only evidence connecting a defendant to a crime consisted of police testimony or a confession made to a police officer. Shapiro didn't trust police testimony uncorroborated by outside evidence. He considered it unreliable, and in some instances untruthful, which was unusual for a judge with a prosecutor's background.

Judge Shapiro's reputation preceded him, and so when I appeared before him for the first time, I came as prepared as possible, not only for my assigned cases, but also for those assigned to my partner as well. In or out of his judicial robe, Shapiro looked like a judge, with a full head of white hair and a stern, commanding presence. "I may not be right, but I'm never in doubt," he often repeated. Without losing any time, the judge directed me to brief him on the pending cases. I could tell by his questions that he was testing my preparation as well as my thinking.

Presently, he asked for the other assistant DA in the trial part, Edward Herman. I explained that he was ill but should be in the following day. Shapiro, anxious to start a trial that was assigned to Herman—a trial in which a father had been accused of raping his eleven-year-old daughter—refused to wait. He directed me to start selecting a jury, as the defense attorney was present and ready to proceed. Herman, the judge promised, could make his opening statement to the jury the following day. Later that day, I returned to my office to learn that Herman would be out several more days. Knowing Judge Shapiro wouldn't adjourn or recess the trial and being familiar with the case, I spent the entire evening preparing the witnesses and researching the law. In my research, I discovered a written opinion by Judge Shapiro in a similar case.

The following day, in my opening statement to the jury, I incorporated some of the language and expressions from his opinion. In my summation to the jury two days later, I actually plagiarized Judge Shapiro's charge dealing with the legal requirements of the testimony of a child of tender years. The result was almost a forgone conclusion, and the jury reached a guilty verdict without prolonged deliberations.

Frank O'Connor sent for me several days later to tell me Judge Shapiro called him to compliment me on my preparation and on the way I had tried the case. When I returned to the courtroom, the judge invited me to join him in his chambers during a court recess. There he advised me to try as many cases as I could. "Each trial is a valuable learning tool; there's no substitute for experience," he told me. "You'll even learn a lot from your opponents, all of whom will use different techniques and approaches. Amassing trials is the best way for you to acquire the perspective and the quickness of thought and decision that trial work requires." It was excellent advice, and I followed it to the letter, trying every case I could, especially those involving violent crimes. The experience stood me in good stead when I faced the biggest challenge of my career: the murders of Kitty Genovese, Barbara Kralik, and Annie Mae Johnson—the cases Frank O'Connor assigned to me on that warm day in April 1964.

CHAPTER TWO

In preparation for the meeting with O'Connor and the others the following morning, I skipped dinner with the family—as I would almost every evening over the next eleven months, putting a strain on everybody—and started looking over the file on the Kralik homicide. The first couple of pages were deeply disturbing, not least because I had two young daughters upstairs. I gritted my teeth and plowed ahead.

Barbara Kralik had been on the verge of entering her junior year of high school in September 1963. Her family lived in the village of Springfield Gardens, in the southern half of Queens, a quiet suburban community of tree-lined streets and one-family homes, largely untouched by the apartment-house invasion that was taking place elsewhere in the borough. A petite, attractive blonde who stood five feet two inches, Barbara was a vivacious girl, popular with her peers in the Girl Scouts, at school, and in her neighborhood. She dated but didn't have a steady boyfriend. Her closest friend was Pat Farfone, who had recently moved from Springfield Gardens to Valley Stream in Nassau County, just over the Queens border. Bosom buddies, the two girls spent as much time as they could together, having frequent sleepovers after Pat moved away.

Barbara was the middle child and only daughter of Joseph and Marie Kralik. They lived with her younger brother, Lawrence, age ten, and her paternal grandmother in a three-bedroom house at the corner of 140th

Avenue and 175th Street. Her older brother was emancipated and lived in his own apartment elsewhere in Queens. Barbara's father, a railway express truck driver, was a hardened Marine Corp veteran who had seen combat at Midway and Okinawa in World War II. Tough as he was, Joseph tried not to be too authoritarian with Barbara. This required little effort on his part, for Barbara respected his wishes and observed the rules he set. Nor was she any trouble to her mother, Marie, a housewife who was suffering from a serious heart problem.

On July 19, 1963, a Friday night, Barbara and Pat made plans for a sleepover in the Kralik home. These plans were known to many of their friends in the neighborhood. At the last minute, however, the sleepover was canceled. Pat decided to spend the weekend in New Jersey with family, and Barbara went to a movie in Jamaica with another girlfriend. This change in plans turned out to be tragic.

Barbara returned home at around ten that night and was already in her pajamas watching television when, half an hour later, her parents and brother came back from an outing of their own. Her parents retreated upstairs to their bedroom, passing the grandmother's bedroom on their way, while Lawrence went to sleep in his room on the ground floor in an enclosed porch at the front of the house. Barbara stayed up. What time she went to sleep is unknown.

Sometime between 2:30 and 3:30 a.m., a lone intruder removed a screen to one of the porch windows, which were open, slipped past the sleeping Lawrence and entered the Kralik home. Gliding up the stairs in pitch-blackness, the person passed the grandmother's room and the parents' room before finally entering Barbara's, which was located at the front of the house. Her bed lay a mere ten feet from her parents' on the other side of the wall.

Barbara was sound asleep, her bedcovers thrown to one side as I discovered from the police photographs in the file that had been taken in the early morning hours of July 20, 1963. It was a dismal, rainy night. With the cloud cover obscuring the moon and trees in full bloom enveloping the nearest streetlight, Barbara's room lay in almost total darkness. Apparently, she must have wakened to see a figure in the room, camouflaged by the darkness. Without a moment to get her bearings, she screamed and was struck in the face as I could clearly see from the autopsy photographs. The blow was obviously followed by violent and repeated stab wounds in the chest and upper abdomen. Moaning, the girl went into shock while her assailant fled, exiting as stealthily as he had entered.

The household was fast asleep. No one saw or heard the intruder. At last, however, Barbara's moans wakened her mother.

"Lawrence, is that you?" Marie called out. There was no answer, and she heard another moan. "Barbara," she yelled, "is that you?" Again, no answer. Marie turned to her husband and shook him awake. "Joseph, Barbara must be having one of her nightmares again!"

They rushed into their daughter's room to find her lying in a pool of blood. How much time had passed since the attack was unclear. Marie's screams woke up Barbara's grandmother and brother, and the household fell into a panic. Marie dashed downstairs to call the police, who arrived within minutes along with an ambulance. By now it was close to 4:00 a.m. Barbara was rushed to Queens General Hospital with Detective Joseph Fullam and a medical technician inside.

"Who did this to you?" the detective asked her.

"It was dark, it was dark," were the only words the girl could get out before losing consciousness. I didn't know it as I studied the file, but Barbara's words would be the subject of bitter legal wrangling in the future.

Upon her arrival at the hospital, Barbara was still alive. For eight hours and forty-five minutes, surgeons operated on her in a desperate effort to save her life, removing her spleen and giving her blood transfusions, but it was to no avail. Barbara had lost too much blood, and her heart wasn't strong enough. Joseph and Marie Kralik's lovely fifteen-year-old daughter died on the operating room table without regaining consciousness and naming or describing her assailant.

The screams of the family had awakened the neighbors, and they gathered outside. They told detectives from the 103rd Detective Squad that no one had heard anything on the street until the yelling came from the Kralik house. Nor had anyone seen anything.

The homicide aroused the police department in Queens as if from a siesta. Inspector Frederick Lussen, chief of detectives, assigned Captain Timothy Dowd, commanding officer of the 16th Detective Division, to direct the investigation and report to him. Dowd immediately assembled a task force to find Barbara's killer. It eventually numbered 130 detectives drawn from Queens's various detective squads. The task force operated out of the 103rd Police Precinct in Jamaica, only a few minutes' drive from Springfield Gardens.

Although Lussen and Dowd agreed every possible lead had to be pursued, they believed the crime had been committed by someone known to the family—someone familiar enough with the household to enter and pass the room of every sleeping member of the family before entering Barbara's room, assaulting her, and leaving undetected. Only a person who had already been in the house would know to enter through an unlocked front porch window and leave through a side door (the front door was stuck and made a loud squeaky noise when opened). Moreover, they believed, this didn't appear to be a random crime; whoever committed it had a reason, however illogical, for bypassing all those rooms and going directly to Barbara's.

On August 28, 1963, following a six-week investigation, Alvin Lewis Mitchell, Pat Farfone's boyfriend and a friend of Barbara's, was arrested. He orally confessed to the murder to Captain Dowd and other police officers and in writing to both Detective John Palmer and Assistant DA Stanley Pryor. Mitchell admitted that on the night of the killing, dressed in a black T-shirt and black jeans, he and his friend, George Borges, had burglarized a school in Fresh Meadows, during which he cut his right hand, wrapping it in a handkerchief. Later, Borges had driven him to the Kralik home to see his girlfriend, Pat Farfone, whom he believed was sleeping over in Barbara's room.

"I took off the screen to one of the front windows and slid into the house," Mitchell confessed. "Without waking anyone, I went upstairs to Barbara's room and thought I saw two people sleeping in the bed. I shook the one I thought was Pat, but it was Barbara. She awoke and started to scream, and I punched her in the face and took out the scissors in my pocket that I had stolen from a school earlier that night and stabbed her a few times and then ran out of the house through the side door. I jumped into the car and told George Borges, let's get the hell out of here, I just stabbed a girl."

Surely, I thought, Mitchell must have panicked when Barbara started to scream, knowing Barbara's battle-hardened father would wake up and come after him.

Mitchell was nineteen years old, tall, slender, and good looking, with sandy-colored hair cut in a wavy pompadour style. A high school dropout, he ran with a gang and had been involved in a number of rumbles. The Monster, as the gang had dubbed him, was known to become violent under the influence of alcohol; he had an assault case pending in criminal court. His employment as an unskilled packer was leading nowhere. Mitchell gave little thought to his future, preferring to spend his free time in Springfield Gardens with other gang members, including Borges, who was three years younger, and his girlfriend Pat Farfone, when her parents permitted. Mitchell had once lived with his parents in Springfield Gardens. Later, the family moved to Astoria, about forty-five minutes by bus and train from Springfield Gardens. Astoria, an ethnically and racially diverse community, was experiencing growing drug and crime problems. To survive on the streets there, young men were expected to display toughness and bravado, and Mitchell was no exception. His closest friends still lived in Springfield Gardens, and he usually returned there on weekends, often staying over at a friend's house where he kept extra clothing.

Under questioning by the police and Assistant DA Pryor, George Borges essentially corroborated Mitchell's version of events. Mitchell was booked on a murder charge and shortly afterward indicted by a Queens County grand jury for murder in the first degree. In addition, he was indicted for burglary of a public school earlier in the evening on which the attack against Barbara took place. Borges was also charged and indicted for the burglary.

I was surprised that not one newspaper article about the crime appeared in the Mitchell file—there had been many, especially of late—

and made a mental note to get a hold of copies of the articles.

Reviewing the Mitchell file, I couldn't help wondering how I would feel if one of my own daughters was murdered in cold blood. Yet I knew I had to maintain a certain detachment in my investigation and preparation. In the interest of justice, I had to remain open-minded, for although Alvin Mitchell had confessed to the crime, serious questions existed in the DA's office as to whether he had actually committed it. The New York media had been exploring and exploiting the question, and I knew I had to be cautious—best not to form any opinion, one way or the other.

CHAPTER THREE

I already knew that questions about Mitchell's culpability had been raised in the Genovese case, but before turning to that file, I opened Annie Mae Johnson's. It was thin, just a few pages describing the circumstances under which her dead body was found, partially burned, in the living room of her home in Jamaica in February 1964. No person had been charged with homicide.

The file included two autopsy reports. The first, prepared by an assistant medical examiner in New York City, concluded that death was the result of multiple stab wounds inflicted by an ice pick. The second, prepared by another medical examiner based on a later autopsy performed in South Carolina, concluded that death was caused by six 22-caliber bullets detected in X-rays taken of the body. The second autopsy was performed after exhuming Annie Mae Johnson's body following serious questions about the cause of her death that were raised in the Genovese case.

The Genovese file was much heftier, consisting of several folders. One described the crime, another the arrest of her killer and his confessions; the third was an analysis of the alleged connection of Kitty's killer to the Kralik and Johnson homicides, and the fourth contained a slew of newspaper articles about the Genovese murder.

At the time of her death, Catherine Genovese was a petite twenty-nine-year-old, little over five feet tall and weighing not much more than one hundred pounds. Raised in Brooklyn by Vincent and Rachel Genovese, she remained behind when her parents moved the family to New Canaan, Connecticut, in 1954.

Kitty and her lover, Mary Ann Zielonko, lived together in an apartment at 82-70 Austin Street in Kew Gardens, Queens. The building, a so-called taxpayer, had stores on the ground floor and small apartments on the top floor. The store entrances were on Austin Street, while the apartments were accessed by way of five separate entrances at the rear of the building, off a walkway adjacent to Long Island Railroad tracks. There were two apartments in Kitty and Mary Ann's entryway.

Kitty and Mary Ann were employed as co-managers of Ev's 11th Hour Bar and Grill in Hollis, Queens, about a twenty-minute drive to the apartment. Employees and customers alike respected them. Kitty had a lively personality, was always upbeat, and loved to dance. Freed from the constraints of her upbringing, she was enjoying her alternative lifestyle and her relationship with Mary Ann.

At about 2:30 a.m. on March 13, 1964, Kitty left the bar alone and drove home in her little red Fiat. Presently, she arrived at the traffic light at Hoover Avenue in Kew Gardens. While waiting for the light to change, she was observed by a man in a white car parked on Hoover Avenue next to the criminal court building. Kitty made a left turn onto Hoover and drove the remaining four blocks home, followed by the white car. She parked her car in the Long Island Railroad parking lot on Austin Street, in front of the closed railroad station. Kitty's stalker parked his car in a corner bus stop on Austin Street, giving himself a clear view of the entire parking lot.

It was a cold, dark night, and the street was deserted. Kitty got out of her car, huddled in a heavy wool coat, and started toward the walkway leading to her apartment. Seconds later, the man, wielding a hunting knife and with a stocking cap pulled over his head, slipped out of his car and began running her way. Apparently Kitty spotted her pursuer, for immediately she turned and made a mad dash up Austin Street toward Lefferts Boulevard, a main thoroughfare one block away.

Unfortunately for Kitty, her stalker was faster. Before she made it to Lefferts Boulevard, the man caught up to her in the middle of the block, directly across the street from the nine-story Marbury apartment building at 82-67 Austin Street. He grabbed hold of her under a streetlight, raised his knife, and began plunging it into her back. She was stabbed four times.

"Help me, help me, I'm being stabbed!" the victim screamed, over and over again.

Her horrifying screams echoed along Austin Street, so pronounced and unmistakable that any person within listening range had to realize the person producing them was in peril. And many did. Kitty's screams alerted or awakened numerous tenants living in the Marbury as well as those in a seven-story apartment building at 82-40 Austin Street. The front of the building faced the bus stop where the killer's white car was parked, and the side of the building was adjacent to the parking lot of the railroad station.

Hearing the screams, tenants in the two apartment buildings began peering out their windows.

At least six of the neighbors witnessed different stages of the attack. One of the neighbors, Robert Mozer, who lived on the seventh floor of the Marbury, was wakened by the screams. He opened his window and "saw this fellow bending over this girl and she was in a kneeling position." Mozer yelled out several times, though in later interviews with investigators he couldn't recall his exact words. Some neighbors heard a male voice yell out, "What's going on down there? What's going on down there?"

Andrée Picq, whose fourth-floor window in the Marbury directly faced the scene of the crime, heard Kitty's screams for help. She told investigators that she'd seen Kitty "lying down on the pavement…she was completely lying down, and a man was bending over her and beating her." After hearing Mozer yell, she saw the attacker run toward the bus stop and saw Kitty get up slowly and stagger toward the back street where the entrance to her apartment was located, all the while screaming for help.

The assistant building supervisor in the Marbury, Joseph Fink, was seated in a chair facing a large bay window with an unobstructed view of the crime scene. Fink watched the vicious assault and heard Kitty's screams for help and Mozer's yells. Instead of taking action, he got up from his chair and took the elevator to his basement quarters to go to sleep. Alongside his bed sat a phone that he could have picked up but didn't.

Hearing Kitty's screams, Samuel Koshkin, who lived on the sixth floor of 82-40 Austin Street, looked out of a side window and saw the killer running down Austin Street toward the bus stop. Koshkin then moved to his front window, which looked out on the bus stop directly below. The tenant saw the killer jump into his white car, back it up to the first residential side street, park, and emerge shortly thereafter with the stocking cap removed, replaced by a fedora. Koshkin saw the killer return to Austin Street. Irene Frost, who lived five floors below Koshkin, also saw the killer returning to Austin Street in a fedora.

During the time her attacker was gone, Kitty staggered to the corner and around the block toward the entryway to her apartment. Irene Frost heard Kitty's continuing shrieks: "Please help me, God. Please help me, I've been stabbed." Kitty never reached her doorway. She was too weak. Still moaning, she collapsed inside the neighboring vestibule at 82-62 Austin Street, midway between her entryway and the railroad station.

The killer searched for Kitty, looking inside the locked railroad station and a closed coffee shop at the corner of the walkway. Then, alerted by her screams—they were still so loud that some of the tenants at the Marbury and 82-40 Austin Street, the building on the far side of the parking lot, could hear them—he headed for the vestibule.

Karl Ross lived in the only apartment at 82-62 Austin Street, only one flight up from where Kitty lay bleeding. His door faced the stairway. Ross opened his door wide enough to see a man leaning over Kitty. The attacker stabbed her at least nine more times, including once in the throat, apparently to silence her. Rather than calling the police, Ross called a girlfriend and asked her what to do. "Don't get involved," she told him. Then he made a second call to Sophie Farrar, Kitty's next-door neighbor, to tell her of Kitty's distress.

Presently, Kitty's attacker left the hallway and ran in the opposite direction from which he had come, taking with him a number of personal articles belonging to his victim, including her billfold and her apartment and car keys.

From the time Kitty's screams were first heard on Austin Street until her stalker left her wounded in Ross's entryway, approximately forty-five minutes passed. Incredibly, during this period not one of Kitty's neighbors called the police or took any action to aid the victim. With but one exception, Sophie Farrar, all the neighbors who had witnessed the attack averted their eyes.

Running up the walkway to Lefferts Boulevard, the attacker made a left turn and another one at Austin Street. He crossed over to the other side and dashed down the street, passing directly in front of the Marbury. On the way back to his car, he was seen by a truck driver, Edward Fiesler, who had just pulled up to deliver milk outside a closed grocery store, a few doors from where Kitty was first assaulted. The attacker returned to his car and immediately left Kew Gardens.

As soon as she received the call from Karl Ross, Sophie Farrar phoned the police, then rushed to the vestibule to find Kitty stretched out on her back, moaning but still alive. Her wool coat was ripped and bloody, her undergarments were cut open, and she was fully exposed. Sophie, a petite woman in her early thirties with a young baby at home, fell to her knees and cradled Kitty in her arms. The police documents confirmed that Sophie was the only person to show concern or compassion for Kitty Genovese during the early morning hours of March 13, 1964.

Kitty Genovese died in the ambulance on the way to Queens General Hospital.

I was already familiar with some of the details of this case from newspaper accounts I had seen. Reading over the contents of the file, however, put it all in a different and more grisly perspective. Sickened by the grim reality of human indifference, all I could do was bury my head in my hands. It was going to be devilishly difficult to maintain any objectivity in a case such as this.

CHAPTER FOUR

The murder of Kitty Genovese occurred within the territorial jurisdiction of the 102nd Queens Detective Squad commanded by Lieutenant Bernard Jacobs. A handsome Dapper Dan, Jacobs was a superb detective and squad commander with a hands-on approach to every investigation his detectives were conducting. His squad, while far from the busiest, was still one of the most successful in Queens, with one of the highest percentages of closed investigations.

Upon his arrival at Austin Street in the early morning hours of March 13, Jacobs ordered his detectives to knock on every door in the two apartment buildings and Kitty's taxpayer. "Wake up every neighbor, and find out what happened," he said. His detectives did as directed, questioning neighbors over the course of two days, and managed to piece together the details of the two attacks on Kitty as well as a general description of her killer.

Apparently he was a light-skinned black man, about twenty-five to thirty years of age, of medium height and slightly built. His car was described only by its color, white. As soon as these details surfaced, a radio alarm went out with the killer's description and that of his car.

Jacob's detectives were all hardened by years of investigating violent crimes. Nonetheless, they were literally shaken, listening to one neighbor after another describe Kitty's screams and admit to not having taken any action. The initial detective reports indicated that about thirty-eight neighbors had heard Kitty's screams, and most of them had witnessed the first attack. It was likely, the detectives believed, that many more people had heard the screams and were simply denying it. The detectives were convinced that had the police been called, the second attack would have been prevented, and Kitty would have survived.

Five days after the murder, on March 18, at about 3:00 p.m., a black male was seen carrying a television set out of the home of Everett Bannister, at 23-34 102nd Street in Corona, Queens, only a few miles from Kew Gardens. A concerned neighbor, Raoul Cleary, approached the man.

"What are you doing in the Bannister's' house?" he asked.

The man answered, "I'm helping them move."

After watching the man load the TV into a white Chevrolet Corvair and return to the Bannister house, Cleary phoned another neighbor, Jack Brown.

"Are the Bannisters moving?" Cleary said.

"Absolutely not," Brown answered, then left his house and met Cleary outside. The man was still inside the Bannister house, they figured, and so Brown left to call the police while Cleary disabled the burglar's car by unhooking the distributor caps. When the man returned to his car and couldn't start it, he left on foot. Moments later, Patrolman Daniel J. Dunn arrived, and Cleary gave him the man's description and pointed out the direction in which he had left. Dunn gave chase and apprehended the man a block away.

Dunn, a well-trained police officer dedicated to law enforcement and crime prevention, had scrupulously noted the police alarm describing Kitty's killer and the color of his car. Realizing the man and his car fit the description in the alarm, Dunn notified detectives from the 102nd Detective Squad. Two detectives promptly arrived, picked the man up, and brought him in for questioning.

His name was Winston Moseley, a resident of South Ozone Park in Queens, a short distance away from the place where he was arrested. With an IQ over 130, he was a twenty-nine-year-old Remington Rand business machine operator, who worked for the Raygram Corporation for ten years in Mount Vernon, New York, a northern suburb of New York City.

Lieutenant Jacobs questioned Moseley with several detectives present as witnesses during the interrogation. Jacobs only raised the issue of Kitty's homicide, his sole interest at this time; at no time did he refer to the burglary for which Moseley had been apprehended. Jacobs knew that merging questions and answers relating to multiple crimes could create problems during a trial. Moseley didn't need prompting. Calmly and without hesitation, almost as if he was having a friendly discussion, he described every detail of the two attacks on Kitty Genovese. Jacobs and his detectives made no written notes, knowing an assistant DA from the Homicide and Investigations Bureau would come and take a detailed typewritten statement from Moseley that he would be asked to sign.

Moseley's description of the crime was so accurate that there could be no question he was the killer. He told the detectives he had left his home in a white Corvair, looking for a lone, unattended woman to rape, rob, and kill. He saw Kitty alone and followed her to the Long Island Railroad station. When she started to run, he said, he overtook her, jumped on her back and stabbed her a number of times. She fell to the ground, and he kneeled over her. Then a man shouted down from an upper floor. Moseley returned to his car, afraid someone would identify his car and license plate. After backing his car into the next cross street, he parked it and changed his hat from a stocking cap to a fedora. He went on to describe in detail his search for the wounded Kitty and finding her in the vestibule where the second attack took place. After exposing his victim by cutting open her clothes, he tried to rape her. His statement included the fact that he had stolen a billfold from Kitty as well as her keys and had discarded them in a parking lot adjacent to his place of employment in Mount Vernon, New York. Detectives would eventually recover the billfold and keys at the location Moseley described, and Mary Ann Zielonko, Kitty's lover, would identify the billfold as belonging to the victim. Mary Ann and Kitty had received identical billfolds as gifts, one black and one brown, which they had exchanged because each one wanted the other color.

After listening to Moseley's oral confession, Jacobs went to report to Queens's chief of detectives, Inspector Frederick Lussen, leaving Moseley in the custody of three detectives. Moseley proceeded to tell them of many crimes he had committed, including several rapes, attempted rapes, several instances of sodomy, and some thirty burglaries.

Suddenly, without even being asked, Moseley volunteered, "I shot a woman, Annie Mae Johnson, six times with a 22-caliber rifle on February 29, 1964. After shooting her on the stoop as she was about to enter her house in South Ozone Park, Queens, I dragged her body inside and attempted to have intercourse with her but couldn't do it as I was impotent. I didn't care if she was alive or dead or who was upstairs in the house, I set fire to her body in the living room, which was only a short distance from where I live in South Ozone Park."

Without taking notes, the three detectives listened to Moseley describe the Johnson killing. When Moseley finished detailing how he had shot Annie Mae Johnson, one of the detectives asked, "Did you really shoot her?" Moseley nodded affirmatively. The detective didn't believe Moseley; he recalled the Johnson autopsy had fixed the cause of death as multiple stabbing by a sharp instrument, an ice pick or something similar.

Suddenly, without thinking, one of the detectives—the file didn't reveal his name—recklessly blurted out, "I bet you also killed that fifteen-year-old girl in Springfield Gardens in July of last year."

"Yeah, I did that one too," Moseley said.

The detectives were taken back. The Kralik case was a closed one, with the defendant, Alvin Mitchell, under indictment. Immediately they put an end to their conversation with Moseley, locked him in a holding cell, and went to report to Lieutenant Jacobs. Jacobs was upset by the report, knowing the effect Moseley's admission to the Kralik murder could have on the Mitchell prosecution. Moseley, he suspected, was clever—clever enough to be preparing for a defense of insanity by confessing to crimes he hadn't committed, such as the Annie Mae Johnson and Barbara Kralik murders.

Winston Moseley was more than clever, having committed over thirty house burglaries and a number of vicious sex crimes without being caught. Married to a twenty-four-year-old registered nurse, Elizabeth, who worked nights at City Hospital in Elmhurst, he would leave their two children unattended in the middle of the night while he went about his ugly business of rape, sodomy, burglary, and murder—or so he told the detectives. The fact that he displayed no emotion or concern for his present circumstances caused Jacobs to believe it was a controlled performance and therefore suspect. The police were convinced he told the truth about Kitty, but not about Annie Mae Johnson or Barbara Kralik. Nonetheless, Jacobs was duty-bound to inform Phillip Chetta, the assistant DA on call from the Homicide and Investigations Bureau. Chetta was one of the most experienced assistant DAs in the bureau.

When Chetta arrived in the squad room, Jacobs called him into his office and described in detail Moseley's admissions concerning the attacks on Kitty Genovese. Next, Jacobs told him about Moseley's statements relating to Annie Mae Johnson and Barbara Kralik. Chetta was irate, knowing it would have a disastrous effect on the Mitchell indictment for the murder of Barbara Kralik. The assistant DA was less concerned with Moseley's claim about Annie Mae Johnson. After all, the Johnson autopsy report fixed multiple stabbing by an ice pick as the cause of death and probable murder weapon, not the 22-caliber rifle Moseley claimed to have used.

As soon as the stenographer arrived, Chetta proceeded with his Q&A of Moseley, limiting it to the details of the Genovese homicide and astutely avoiding any reference to Johnson or Kralik. Like Jacobs, Chetta didn't want to compromise Moseley's confession to the murder of Kitty Genovese. By the end of the session, Chetta was satisfied that Moseley had in fact killed Kitty Genovese.

Still concerned about the effect Moseley's claims relating to Annie Mae Johnson and Barbara Kralik might have on the prosecution of Mitchell, Chetta contacted Bernard Patten, chief of the DA Homicide and Investigations Bureau. Patten had already been informed of the arrest and confession by Moseley to the murder of Genovese. Chetta reached Patten by phone at his home.

"We have a serious problem with the Mitchell case," he said. "Moseley has also confessed to killing Barbara Kralik. It's probably baloney, because he also claims he shot Annie Mae Johnson to death in February, and we know she was stabbed to death. How do you want me to handle it?"

"Don't question him, and don't take any statements about the Johnson and Kralik homicides," Patten answered. "I'm going to call O'Connor and discuss it with him."

Patten told O'Connor everything Chetta had discussed with him. At first, O'Connor was silent. Then he said, "Let's have a meeting in my office tomorrow morning. I want you, Chetta, and Cacciatore there. We have to decide how to handle this. If we discredit Moseley's statement that he killed the Johnson woman, we might be able to discount his statement that he killed the Kralik girl."

Bernard Patten, who had an almost professorial air, was an outstanding bureau chief, thorough in his attention to detail and possessing the technical and legal knowledge to evaluate any kind of homicide case. O'Connor's reliance on his recommendations was well placed. They were friends of many years, trusted one another, and could read each other's minds.

The meeting started in the early morning of March 19, 1964, with a briefing by Chetta. The men decided that although Moseley's confessions to the Johnson and Kralik murders were highly questionable, the statements couldn't be passed over lightly. They would have to be thoroughly investigated, and the investigation would have to be completed before Mitchell's trial could proceed.

"Barney," O'Connor told Patten, "you and your staff handle the investigation, and keep the police out of it. I'm concerned the police questioning of Moseley may have compromised the Mitchell case. This isn't nearly as upsetting to me as the possibility that Mitchell is innocent and the entire police investigation leading to his arrest and indictment is corrupt. I don't want a second wrong-man case in Queens when I'm the prosecutor rather than the defense attorney."

Another broader concern of O'Connor's was that a corrupt police investigation would affect other indictments pending in his jurisdiction.

"Why doesn't my bureau start with Annie Mae Johnson?" Patten suggested. "Refuting Moseley's statement about shooting her to death will help destroy his credibility with respect to the Kralik confession."

There had been no information in the media about the cause of Annie Mae Johnson's death, and Moseley couldn't have detailed knowledge about it unless he was the killer. Patten and O'Connor hoped they could resolve the problem of the two confessions without media meddling, which would complicate the Mitchell prosecution. Unfortunately, this wasn't to be.

Three days after their meeting, on March 22, 1964, New York City's largest-circulation tabloid, the *New York Daily News*, ran an article with the headline "Two Admit Same Slaying, Baffle Cops." It not only included the two confessions, but also reported that Moseley's confession contained details about the killing of Barbara Kralik that only her killer could have known. Whatever the source of the article—it was never discovered—the genie was out of the bottle. The very next day, the *Daily News*, the *New York Post*, and other city papers carried follow-up articles, adding phony statements claimed to have been made by Barbara Kralik. "I woke up when I felt a thump on my stomach," the *Daily News* quoted the victim as saying on the verge of death. "I saw this fellow leaning over me, and I screamed. I never saw him before in my life." According to both the *News* and the *Post*, Barbara Kralik described her assailant as a white man with dark skin. The articles thereafter described Mitchell as fair skinned and Moseley as a light-skinned Negro.

The tabloids were making up stories. As far as I knew, Detective Fullam was the only person to speak to Barbara after the attack, and all she had said before lapsing into unconsciousness was, "It was dark, it was dark."

In a note contained in the case file, Patten speculated that the false information was planted by Herbert Lyon, Mitchell's defense attorney. Now Mitchell was claiming innocence.

Then again, maybe the tabloids weren't lying. I wondered why copies of these newspaper articles weren't in the Mitchell file and made a memo to myself to investigate every aspect of Barbara Kralik's last hours so as to confirm her last remark to Detective Fullam. In view of the *Daily News* article, I had to be absolutely certain that no other words had been uttered by Barbara to anyone. The truth left no margin for error.

Following their meeting with O'Connor, Patten and Chetta had reviewed all the material in the slim file on Annie Mae Johnson. The file contained nothing but an incomplete police report. Puzzled that the autopsy report was missing, Patten called the medical examiner's office and sent a detective to retrieve it. After receiving the autopsy report, Patten learned that Annie Mae Johnson had been buried in South Carolina, and he directed Chetta, along with Dr. James Furey, an assistant medical examiner, to go to South Carolina to exhume and X-ray the body. When they got off the train in Monk's Corner, South Carolina, the local coroner was sarcastically flipping a bullet in his hand in a show of one-upmanship. Apparently he had already X-rayed the body and extracted six 22-caliber bullets embedded in the victim's muscle fascia.

Chetta was shaken. Until those X-rays were taken and the six 22-caliber bullets recovered, the only person who could have known that Annie Mae Johnson had been shot six times with a 22-caliber rifle was her killer. If Moseley's confession about Johnson was true, as it now appeared, perhaps his claim about having killed Barbara Kralik was also true. Perhaps Mitchell *was* innocent.

Without losing any time, Chetta put a call in to Patten, who hurried over to Frank O'Connor's office with the news. Usually calm, even in the midst of campaigns for public office, O'Connor lost his temper this time. "I'll consider a dismissal of the indictment charging Mitchell with murder," he said.

"That's premature, Frank. I suggest we discuss the situation with Frank Cacciatore and get his opinion."

While O'Connor pondered what to do about the Mitchell case, press coverage of the Kitty Genovese case heated up. *New York Times* Editor A. M. Rosenthal, who had learned about the failure of Kitty's neighbors to come to her aid, directed Martin Gansberg, one of his investigative reporters, to look deeper into the crime. Gansberg's investigation produced a front-page article on March 27, 1964, titled "Thirty-Seven Who Saw Murder Didn't Call the Police." Although in error about the number of attacks and the number of neighbors who allegedly saw them take place, the article did vividly describe Kitty's screams during the first attack and the indifference of her neighbors. Clearly Gansberg had spoken to some of the neighbors.

The article stirred public outrage. Overnight, Kew Gardens became dirty words, and Kitty's neighbors were excoriated for their inhuman response to her tragedy. The media descended on Kew Gardens in a mad frenzy, interviewing neighbors without any concern that their actions might compromise the prosecution. Reporters knocked on every door in the two apartment buildings and taxpayer. The response, however, was disappointing. Many of the neighbors, either too ashamed to speak or hoping to avoid notoriety had become closemouthed about the events of March 13.

Fortunately for the prosecution, reporters didn't have access to the police detectives' interviews naming neighbors who had initially admitted seeing the attack or hearing the screams. As a result, certain details of the crime remained out of the public eye.

Within a few days of his arrest, Winston Moseley was formally charged with killing Kitty Genovese. Without delay, he was indicted by a grand jury and charged with murder in the first degree, punishable, if a jury so determined, by death. Three attorneys were appointed for Moseley: Sidney Sparrow, Martha Zelman, and Sidney Liss. Sparrow, the busiest and arguably the most competent criminal defense attorney in Queens, was lead attorney. The defense team promptly made application to Judge Shapiro for a psychiatric evaluation of Moseley to determine if he was mentally competent to stand trial. Did Moseley understand the nature of the charges against him? Was he able to assist in his defense? Two forensic psychiatrists at Kings County Hospital determined after examining Moseley that he was schizophrenic. But insanity wasn't the issue—the issue was whether he was competent to stand trial, and the answer was yes. Winston Moseley would stand trial for the horrendous murder to which he had confessed.

CHAPTER FIVE

It was well after midnight when I completed reading through the voluminous Genovese file. To the shock I'd felt when first assigned to the three cases was now added a sense of foreboding, and not a little bit of confusion. Was I really being assigned to these cases for the reasons O'Connor stated, because they were high-profile homicides, and I could use the experience—or was I being thrown to the wolves for a losing cause in the Kralik homicide? After all, who could expect a conviction when two individuals had both confessed to the same crime? I made up my mind to ask Frank Cacciatore if I could be relieved in the Mitchell case. If I couldn't, my hope was that an acquittal would be blamed on the dual confessions and not on any blunder I might make in prosecuting Mitchell's trial.

At the next day's meeting, I had to speak with the utmost candor in expressing my concerns. No doubt O'Connor, with his wrong-man complex, would be quite vocal.

I arrived at the DA's office early the following morning, well before the scheduled meeting, and went directly to Cacciatore's office on the first floor. He looked a little nervous, pacing back and forth behind his desk, almost as if he knew what I was going to say. "Did you go over the files last night?" he asked.

I nodded. "I'm not sure I even want to try the Mitchell case. Even if

Mitchell is guilty, I don't see any chance of winning it. How do you think I should approach this meeting with O'Connor?"

"Don't be afraid to tell him how you feel," Cacciatore replied. "But don't under any circumstances ask to be taken off the case. You have O'Connor's respect now. Don't lose it. You should never be afraid to prosecute any case, provided you believe in the defendant's guilt. You may not realize it, but you really are the right person for the Mitchell case, and you and Judge Shapiro are a good mix. More important, you can do the kind of investigation the case requires. Listen, you're going to work with me on the Moseley case. We'll prepare it together. You have to be prepared to handle it on your own if my appointment to the criminal court comes through. It's a once in a lifetime case, Charlie. You'll be under a microscope, so what? Ask out on Mitchell, and you'll be out on Moseley."

I trusted Cacciatore. He had become my mentor in the office, and in many ways he reminded me of my father, honest and upright. Frank Cacciatore would never steer me in the wrong direction. "Okay," I said, "but try and buy me enough time so that I can do the kind of investigation necessary to be certain of Mitchell's guilt—provided O'Connor decides to go ahead with the trial."

We left Cacciatore's office and went up to the meeting with O'Connor and Patten. Patten gave us a detailed briefing on the Mitchell and Moseley confessions. "We can't discount the possibility of Mitchell's innocence," he said. "Moseley's confession to shooting Johnson is without question true. Why wouldn't his confession to killing Barbara Kralik also be true?"

"Simple," I answered. "Moseley confessed to the Kralik murder to support a defense of insanity. He's a very bright guy with a high IQ. By confessing to a crime he didn't commit, he's protecting himself by setting up his defense."

O'Connor leaned forward in his chair, pointing at a newspaper clipping on his desk. Carefully choosing his words, he said, "I'm deeply concerned about the possible innocence of Alvin Mitchell and won't make any decision on whether to proceed with his trial until you finish your investigation and preparation, Charlie. Our office will face a myriad of problems in the event Mitchell's confession and Borges's statements turn out to be false. False confessions and statements are the result of threats, extortion, or outright brutality; they cannot and will not be tolerated, even if it means indicting every police officer involved with obstructing justice and other crimes. A false confession could easily affect every pending case—and could overturn convictions we've already obtained, notwithstanding the guilt of the defendants."

O'Connor paused, looking each of us in the eye. "I don't want the outstanding record of this office soiled by one case, and this could easily happen. You have to be extremely careful and thoroughly prepared. I want you to find the truth."

"We should try the Moseley case first, then," Cacciatore suggested. "We may learn things during that trial that will help us ferret out Barbara Kralik's true killer. We have time to prepare the Moseley case. Let Charlie work on the Kralik killing for a while before we start preparing the Moseley case. Perhaps he can come up with something. Furthermore, I believe Moseley will testify in his own trial—he'll get up on the witness stand and admit every violent crime he ever committed so the jury will believe he's insane. Then we can cross-examine him about the Kralik homicide and establish the inconsistencies between his version and what really happened."

O'Connor closed the meeting by agreeing to go with the Moseley case first. "I'll keep my options open until after that trial," he concluded. "Before you begin the Mitchell trial, we'll meet again. I expect recommendations from each of you before I make any decision. In the meantime, I want to be kept up to date on everything, including the details of your investigation and preparation, Charlie—especially after you've spoken to any key witness connected to either confession."

With O'Connor's last remark hanging over me, I left the meeting. Clearly, what happened with the two cases could have a profound effect on the Chief's political career, possibly destroying any chance he would have to be the Democratic Party standard bearer in the next gubernatorial election. His ambition of running against Nelson Rockefeller was common knowledge in the office and in the press.

After the meeting, I spoke confidentially with Cacciatore. "I don't know whether to thank Shapiro or curse him for his recommendations. I hope I'm not a sacrificial lamb being led to the slaughter. Can you imagine how the press will handle the fact that Mitchell will be the first murder case I'm trying as lead counsel?"

"You have nothing to lose, Charlie," Cacciatore assured me again. "If you find out from your investigation that Mitchell's confession is false, you'll clear an innocent boy, and if you find out it's true, you'll have a chance to get justice for Barbara Kralik and her family. Nobody expects you to get a conviction, and if you do, you'll vindicate the police and our office. Of course, you may never find out the truth. Just be as well prepared as you have been in your other cases, and you'll be okay." He gave me a pat on the back. "The Chief will back you to the hilt as long as you're straight with him."

While Cacciatore's words were supportive, I knew I had mountains to climb. I still didn't realize how high they would be or how long it would take to scale them.

As I thought over the meeting, I came to believe that pursuing the Mitchell trial was indeed the safest way out for O'Connor and his office. If O'Connor were to dismiss the case, he would in effect be admitting he didn't have faith in the police investigation or in his own assistant DA, Stanley Pryor. It would open a Pandora's box, compromising previous convictions and endangering future cases. If the case went to trial and a jury found Mitchell not guilty, it wouldn't sully the police investigation. The jury would only be saying that two men confessing to the same crime created enough reasonable doubt to require that Mitchell be acquitted. Indeed, such a verdict might relieve our office's burden and transfer it to the medical examiner for the botched autopsy of Annie Mae Johnson.

The Moseley trial was a little over a month away, and Cacciatore told me we would start preparing for it in two weeks. That gave me a mere two weeks to work on the Mitchell prosecution, to interview witnesses, and to take the police investigation apart, piece by piece. And unless O'Connor decided not to prosecute Mitchell, that trial would follow close on the heels of the Moseley trial. I had my work cut out for me.

One of our DA's police detectives, Jack Peters, was assigned to me full time. It was a stroke of luck. A man of quick wit and high integrity, Jack was dedicated to the DA's office and the New York City Police Department, and although our investigation could wind up putting the police department on trial, that fact wouldn't affect his efforts or our investigation and preparation.

Jack and I worked almost around the clock, starting the first morning with Assistant DA Chetta to learn everything we could about Moseley's confession to killing Barbara Kralik. Chetta added little to the information I already had. He had made every effort to find out which detective had put the question to Moseley about Kralik's murder, but the detectives stonewalled him. Chetta was a competent investigating prosecutor. Although the Genovese murder was his prime concern, had he known that Moseley's confession to killing Annie Mae Johnson was true, he certainly would have questioned Moseley in detail about the attack on Barbara Kralik and possibly discovered substantial discrepancies to knock out his confession. But there was no way Chetta could have known that the Johnson autopsy was so thoroughly flawed.

Next, Jack and I turned to Assistant DA Stanley Pryor, who had taken Mitchell's and Borges's typewritten statements. A hard-nosed prosecutor, he told me emphatically that he believed their statements to be true. "I didn't see anything in the precinct that night to suggest otherwise. Both Mitchell and Borges looked like they were happy to get it off their chests."

I wasn't surprised by his remarks. Had it been otherwise, Pryor would certainly have disclosed the problem to Bernard Patten long before speaking to me. Still, there was one problem with Pryor's actions that night, and I was almost angry when I questioned him about it.

"Why in God's name did you stop Mitchell's questioning to go to the bathroom?" I said. "Couldn't you have waited until the Q&A was over? Didn't you realize this would open the door to all sorts of wild claims by defense counsel? Herbert Lyon's going to argue that you stopped the questioning because you didn't like the answers you were getting—that you left the room so the detectives could intimidate Mitchell."

"That's pure baloney," he snapped. "I had to go to the bathroom and was only gone a few minutes. Remember, I didn't take a break when I questioned Mitchell orally, before starting the Q&A."

There was nothing in Pryor's remarks that added to my efforts to determine the truth. I warned him to anticipate a rough cross-examination by the defense counsel or, if the Chief decided to dismiss Mitchell's indictment, an onslaught of abuse at the hands of the media and defense attorneys. Pryor understood the situation, having already been subjected to intense grilling by Bernard Patten.

After meeting with the stenographer who had taken Mitchell's and Borges's statements, Jack and I began delving into the police investigation. Captain Timothy Dowd, who had directed the investigation, was first on my list of police interviewees. I decided to meet with him alone, sans Jack, thinking he'd speak more freely without a subordinate detective from his bureau in the room.

Timothy Dowd, who years later would head the investigation that resulted in the arrest and conviction of serial killer David Berkowitz, the Son of Sam, was a handsome, methodical, and studious person. What appeared to be a gentle nature disguised a steely toughness derived from years of overseeing police investigations. He'd started in the uniformed ranks and all the while continued his education, which culminated in a postgraduate degree in police science. Dowd was confident that painstaking detective work—interviewing every person no matter how remotely connected to Barbara Kralik and following every lead no matter how inconsequential—would eventually lead to the apprehension of her murderer. His determination to find Barbara's killer was heightened by the fact that his wife was expecting a child soon.

Confrontation with Dowd wasn't something I was looking for. It wouldn't crack the door to the truth, and at any rate, I was a neophyte compared to the captain, whose experience with criminal investigations far surpassed mine. No, I would have to work together with him if, assuming Moseley's confession was a red herring, we were to prove Mitchell's guilt. And I had every reason to believe Dowd would work with me. After all, he was in a more precarious situation than I. It was his investigation that was in jeopardy. He and every key detective in his investigating task force in the Kralik case could face criminal prosecution if evidence was discovered proving Mitchell's confession had been obtained under duress.

Still, I wasn't prepared for just how open he was. We hadn't even exchanged pleasantries when he said to me, "Look, I know where you're coming from, and I realize what you want from me. I'll hold nothing back, and my officers won't either; if they do, I'll have their shields and help you prosecute them. The Moseley confession is pure B.S. He couldn't have killed the Kralik girl. My investigation was clean. So fire away, and don't be afraid to hurt my feelings."

His words were so disarming that I decided to be as frank and uninhibited as possible in questioning Dowd and his detectives. After thanking him for being so forthright, I explained that with the two conflicting confessions, even if Mitchell's were true, obtaining a conviction would be difficult, perhaps impossible. It could be a blow to Dowd as the responsible police officer, to the department, and to the DA's office.

"If the case has to blow up," I said, "better it be in my office than in the courtroom, in the presence of an already hostile press." Telling him I was pressed for time, I said every one of his detectives had to be available whenever and wherever I needed them.

He readily agreed, and we were off to a good start. All the next day and late into the night, he filled me in on every last detail of the police investigation. I found him likable, warm, and articulate and hoped my reaction wasn't the product of naiveté or inexperience. Surely he wasn't trying to con me.

"I kept an open mind about the Kralik homicide until the very night Borges and Mitchell decided to tell the truth," Dowd said. "My detectives and I had had Mitchell in for questioning only five times between the homicide and the night he confessed. We gave him every opportunity to tell us how he got back to Astoria that night. Each time we got a different story. We checked each one out, and nothing meshed."

"There were no threats or intimidation, physical or otherwise. If there were, would we have let him out of the station with the bruises? If we wanted to frame him with a phony confession, we would have done it the first night in the stationhouse, when he admitted to the school burglary, and he would never have walked out that night without confessing. But that's not my way and never will be."

He reminded me that Barbara's murder had to have been committed by someone familiar with the house, and that the perpetrator had to have had a reason for going there. "This crime doesn't fit Moseley's pattern," he insisted. "He would never have entered a house under these circumstances. He only attacked women when they were alone, unprotected by men. He couldn't have been sufficiently familiar with that house to enter it and get to Barbara's room without waking someone."

Dowd made a point of telling me that the morning after Mitchell and Borges's statements, he and Mitchell, together with the police detectives and assistant DA Pryor, had gone to the Kralik house for a reenactment. When they approached the house, Mitchell corrected his confession. According to Dowd, Mitchell said, "I told you in the precinct I slid in through the second window, but looking at the house, it was the third window, which wasn't blocked by any bushes."

"Pryor was right there when Mitchell said that. Do you really believe we would have forced Mitchell to make that change with an assistant DA present?" Dowd asked.

I went over every detail of Dowd's investigation with him and concentrated on each of the days he had questioned Mitchell, including once when Mitchell had shown up at the precinct on his own without being asked to come.

It was close to midnight when I finished my first go-round with Dowd. I intended to talk with him again after speaking to some of his detectives.

The next day was devoted to John Palmer, the detective carrying the case from beginning to end. A youthful-looking man with a ruddy complexion, Palmer was responsible for handling the police file and controlling the accused after his arrest. I had never met him, but prior to our meeting, his DD5s (reports of police activity) and the handwritten statements he'd taken from Mitchell and Borges did give me insight into the kind of professional he was. Palmer was so thorough and accurate that he never relied on briefings from other detectives, preferring to verify facts and information independently. Palmer described his participation in the investigation, which closely followed his DD5s, and showed me the personal notes he'd made during the course of the investigation.

After reporting to O'Connor, I went home and compared the notes I'd taken during my talks with Dowd and Palmer. If the investigation was faulty, it had to start and end with these two men, but so far I couldn't find any holes in what they'd told me. There was no deviation in the chronology from either, and more important, neither man hesitated when describing the details of their investigation. Furthermore, everything they'd said fit in with all that I had learned from Assistant DA Stanley Pryor. It just didn't seem possible that the police investigation leading to the arrest of Mitchell was manufactured. Building a false case would have had to involve every detective active in the investigation, and there were 130 in all.

I went to see O'Connor the following morning and told him why I didn't believe the police investigation was a fabrication. He sent for Frank Cacciatore and Bernard Patten, and after I repeated what I had told O'Connor, he asked each of us to make a recommendation. All of us came to the same conclusion: that Mitchell be tried immediately following the Moseley trial. O'Connor, who still had reservations about going ahead with Mitchell's prosecution, reluctantly agreed. I was relieved to hear Cacciatore and Patten make the same recommendation I had. It vindicated my opinion and evaluation of the Mitchell case.

With only a week and a half remaining before putting the Mitchell case on hold, I had Jack Peters schedule every possible witness. I decided that he and I would question the witnesses during the day and that I would prepare the legal issues in the evening in the DA's library.

It was essential that I find the person who told Alvin Mitchell that Pat Farfone was to sleep at Barbara's house on the night of the killing. All I had so far were Mitchell's admissions that he knew of the sleepover. I wanted proof from another source, because it would bolster Mitchell's confession.

45

My first witness was Pat Farfone. A petite, dark-haired, pretty girl, she was clearly upset as she entered my office, almost on the verge of tears. I had detailed notes of her interviews with Dowd and other detectives, and rather than rehashing questions, I appealed to the guilt she felt over the death of her friend. She started to cry, and I tried to calm her, telling her she had nothing to fear, that I was only looking for information to get at the truth. I told her to relax for a few minutes and left her in my office to speak to her parents, who were waiting outside.

"I spent months trying to find out if Pat had told Mitchell about the sleepover," Mr. Farfone told me. "My wife and I are convinced she didn't." Apparently, they had done some investigating of their own, speaking to Pat's friends to find out who told Mitchell about the sleepover, trying to learn if their daughter was telling the truth. "After all," he said, "it could have been our own daughter who was murdered that night."

They did add an important piece of information that the detectives hadn't yet unearthed. While Pat and Alvin had engaged in heavy petting, they hadn't been sexually intimate, though Alvin had pressed Pat on the subject.

During Dowd's questioning of Mitchell, the latter had claimed he'd wanted to go to Barbara's house "to get laid."

"I'll have to ask Pat about this," I warned her parents, and they had no objections.

When I returned to my office, I told Pat I wanted to know everything about her relationship with Mitchell, no matter how embarrassing. Was Mitchell pressing her to have intercourse, and had the pressure increased about the time of Barbara's murder? She said yes, there was pressure and that it had been heavy in early July.

"The only way to put him off was to help him be satisfied without doing it," she managed to tell me.

This information, along with Mitchell's statement to Dowd, offered some measure of explanation for his wanting to see Pat on the night of the murder. Whether I would ask her about it on direct examination during the trial, however, was up in the air. Testimony from a fifteen-year-old girl in her emotional state, in a crowded courtroom, and in the presence of a jury, could hurt rather than help.

The rest of the day was spent in interviews with other friends of Barbara and Pat's. Several believed Mitchell knew of the sleepover, but none could recall any conversations with Mitchell in which he specifically mentioned it. They merely said that everyone in the neighborhood knew about it. As a result of these interviews, I decided not to call any of the girls' friends as witnesses. After all, testimony that everyone in the neighborhood knew about the sleepover was a conclusion not directly connected to Mitchell. Defense counsel would surely object to it, and the objection would be sustained. Furthermore, it would allow defense counsel to call attention to my failure to prove this point through a disinterested witness. And as prosecutor, I couldn't afford to let failures creep into my presentation before the jury.

"Have you given any thought to major problems outside of the Moseley confession?" O'Connor asked the next time I reported to him.

"Yes," I replied. "Barbara's statement in the ambulance on the way to the hospital: 'It was dark, it was dark.' Defense counsel is bound to claim the statement is a description of her assailant—which doesn't necessarily refer to Barbara's inability to see in the darkness. Mitchell is light skinned with wavy blonde hair. Another problem is Pryor's break during the Q&A. The defense is likely to argue the Q&A was stopped because Pryor wasn't happy with the answers he was getting."

Another thing that could complicate matters, I told him, was the fact the Supreme Court of the United States was expected to hand down a decision establishing a new legal requirement during a jury trial for determining whether a confession was voluntary. It was impossible to anticipate how such a decision could affect the trial. Mitchell's statements were sure to be attacked on this ground.

I had been casting about for a general approach to prosecution that would stand me in good stead in my upcoming trials as well as in trials farther down the road. The Chief had devised his own approach over the years, a set of principles that guided his conduct in the courtroom, as had Frank Cacciatore and Judge Shapiro. During my conversation with O'Connor, I finally began to shape mine.

The system was adversarial. Herbert Lyons would be arguing Mitchell's innocence while I would be prosecuting on behalf of the People of the State of New York. If I believed our case was truthful and based on sufficient evidence to submit to a jury, then it was up to the jurors to determine guilt or innocence. It was their responsibility, not mine. I couldn't get sidetracked worrying about a not-guilty verdict or any defense claim that I was bending the facts. After all, I wasn't a witness to the crime or the police investigation. If I had any evidence favorable to the defense, I was obligated to disclose it, and I would try my best to discover any exculpatory evidence. Beyond that, Mitchell's fate was out of my hands. Nor could I lose sleep over the outcome for the police department and any impact on O'Connor's future.

The new approach cleared away the cobwebs, and it was with a new sense of focus that I met the chief medical examiner in Queens, Dr. Richard Grimes, in my office the next morning. The subject quickly turned to a pair of scissors the police had recovered from Mitchell's home—the scissors he had stolen from the school that he and Borges had burglarized on the night of the murder. It was identical to a second pair of scissors, also stolen from the school, that Mitchell told the detectives he had thrown away and that could have been the actual murder weapon.

"Scissors of this type could have produced the wounds I observed on Barbara's body," Grimes said.

"Could a knife have been the murder weapon?"

"It depends on the knife. The wounds have an ovoid shape. I suggest you learn as much detail as you can about the knife Moseley claimed he used to kill Barbara. I might be able to rule it out as a possible murder weapon. For example, a serrated knife couldn't have caused Barbara's wounds."

I paused, trying to phrase the next question as diplomatically as possible. But there was no way to be diplomatic. "Can you tell me about the blunder your assistant medical examiner made in the Johnson autopsy?"

Grimes grew red faced. It was obviously an embarrassment to him, and he tried to explain. "The bullets were embedded in such a way in the muscle fascia that only an X-ray could locate them, not the naked eye. Unless the fascia was literally sliced by machine, the bullets couldn't be found, and at the time, we didn't usually perform autopsies that way."

Though tempted to blurt out my opinion of his assistant medical examiner, I held my tongue. After all, I needed Dr. Grimes. He was an important witness, and without his testimony on the possible cause of Kralik's death, the judge would dismiss the case before a jury had a chance to deliberate.

The rest of the day and for the next week, I worked meticulously with Dowd, Palmer, and the other detectives who had been the most active in the police investigation. Time was short—I couldn't consult those on the periphery—but it wasn't wasted. Everything I learned that week was consistent with what I had begun to believe: Mitchell's confession was voluntary and truthful. Of course, my conviction didn't minimize the difficulty of proving this.

CHAPTER SIX

One day Cacciatore called to tell me he was ready to start preparing the Moseley case. "I need you right away," Frank said. I wanted more time to work with the written material in the Mitchell file. Realizing, however, that Moseley's confession about Barbara was a key to the Mitchell trial, I didn't put up an argument. Instead, I dropped everything and moved into Cacciatore's office.

Our first step in preparing the Moseley case was to see what it really involved. There was little question in my mind that Moseley would be found guilty. The challenges in this case were whether he could get the death penalty and whether Frank and I would get the testimony I needed to prove later that Alvin Mitchell, and not Moseley, was Barbara's killer. We both agreed to concentrate on the known facts and not be too diverted by the question of why the neighbors failed to react to the attack on Kitty Genovese. Of course, we were concerned about the question. After all, we were human beings and like many in the public, we believed that had the police been called during the first attack, Kitty would have survived. As prosecutors, too, we had often been frustrated by the lack of cooperation from witnesses; that would surely be a problem in this case as well. We also understood that jurors might transfer some of the hostility they felt toward Moseley to any neighbors who testified. We wanted their hostility reserved for Moseley alone, since we were pursuing the death penalty for him.

O'Connor never directed us to pursue the death penalty. We simply prepared the trial as if a death penalty phase was the normal course after a guilty verdict of murder in the first degree.

At his arraignment, Moseley's three attorneys, Sidney Sparrow, Sidney Liss, and Martha Zelman, had entered a plea of not guilty. For some strange reason, they failed to enter a plea of not guilty by reason of insanity. Moseley, it will be recalled, had been found mentally competent to stand trial. A defense of insanity, however, was a different issue, and the psychiatric reports had disclosed that Moseley had schizophrenia. We had to assume that the attorneys might change their tune during the trial—that they would obtain permission from Judge Shapiro to pursue an insanity defense. Thus we needed to prepare for two defenses: insanity and an outright denial that Moseley killed Kitty. The possibility of a denial defense meant that Frank and I had to go over what the neighbors heard or saw the night of the attacks—not every neighbor, only those who had seen or heard enough to reconstruct the sequence of events or describe the viciousness of the attacks and those able to connect Moseley to them. We decided to interview approximately twenty neighbors.

Interviewing them raised a logistical question. The media had laid siege to the courthouse and DA wing, and we knew they would dig for every tidbit of information about any neighbor whom they discovered was a prospective witness. We didn't want a repeat of the situation after the *New York Times* story broke, when reporters had hounded the neighbors and meticulously questioned them. And so to protect our interviewees and guard their identity, we gave detailed instructions to Detective Jack Peters and his aides to throw a cordon around each person brought in for questioning. One after another the neighbors were brought in through O'Connor's secure garage entrance to the building.

We spent an entire week with them, questioning, probing, evaluating, and finally determining which people to call to the witness stand. Those were grueling days. Though most of the neighbors' names now escape me, their faces and what they told us are haunting memories, never to be forgotten. Frank and I may have decided not to get sidetracked by the neighbors' passivity, and we may have hidden our emotions during these interviews, but we couldn't help feeling anger. It was all I could do to keep from shouting, "Don't you know that each of us is our brother's keeper?"

We asked two basic questions: what did you hear, and what did you see?

The first person we spoke to was in all likelihood the first to become aware of Kitty's distress: Joseph Fink, the night elevator operator and assistant superintendent of the Marbury apartment building. He'd had an unobstructed view of the attack from his chair looking out across the street through the bay window and was able to identify Moseley. He heard Kitty's screams, and he watched Moseley plunge the knife with its shiny blade into her back. "I thought about going downstairs to get my baseball bat," Fink volunteered, but we knew the thought never entered his head. If he'd been so concerned, why wouldn't he have at least picked up the phone? Instead, he finally admitted, his only action after Moseley ran away and Kitty was bleeding in the street was to get up from his chair, take the elevator downstairs, and go to sleep.

Fink was in his late thirties and appeared relatively strong. The least he could have done, I thought, was open the front door to the apartment building, yell out, "The police are coming!" and lock the door again. This would have protected him from danger and might have stopped the attacker in his tracks. It made me almost sick to my stomach dealing with this man, but as a prosecutor preparing a case, I couldn't afford to get personally involved.

Fink's description of Moseley was the most detailed and accurate one obtained during the police investigation. In the end, however, Frank and I decided not to call him as a witness. It was a difficult decision, made in the interest of keeping jurors' minds concentrated on Moseley's vicious attack, not Fink's inhumanity.

We didn't tell Fink we weren't going to call him. Instead, we gave him a subpoena and told him to be ready to testify at a moment's notice. It was our woefully inadequate attempt at justice. Making him sweat about being called was the most we could do to upset him. He certainly deserved a lot more than that.

The next witness we interviewed was Kitty's neighbor in the taxpayer, Karl Ross, in whose vestibule Kitty had collapsed and where Moseley finished her off. Thin, with balding hair, Ross was an artist by trade. Ross lived alone and had a girlfriend nearby, the one he'd called who told him not to get involved. According to the DD5s, he was wakened by Kitty's screams at the start of the first attack. He gave us a different version: that he first heard Kitty's screams when she was lying on the floor of his entranceway. The DD5s had to be accurate, as Ross's bedroom window faced Austin Street, one flight up and almost directly above the location where Moseley first stabbed Kitty, a distance of no more than thirty feet. His window was closer than any other neighbor's to the site of the first attack.

Ross continued to deny, as he had to the police, that he'd seen Moseley during the attack in the entranceway. We knew he was lying, because Moseley told Jacobs that he heard the door upstairs open and close two or three times, and Ross admitted telling his girlfriend that Kitty was being attacked, asking her what to do. It was impossible to decide who was more despicable, Fink or Ross. Of all the neighbors, they were the best positioned, during the critical moments of Kitty's ordeal, to take action without inviting any harm to themselves. At least Fink wasn't an outright liar. How we would have enjoyed putting Ross before the grand jury to trap him into a charge of perjury! But this route wasn't available to us. Ross, a man who would do anything to avoid accepting responsibility, might foul up our prosecution with his fabrications.

We decided not to call Ross to the stand, not only because he was a liar but also because, as with Fink, we wanted to keep jurors' minds concentrated on Moseley's vicious attack. We did contemplate disclosing Fink's and Ross's identities and addresses to the media, but we were too busy to engage in retribution on Kitty's behalf.

The other neighbors added little useful information. Their lack of action on the night of March 13, 1964, was variously explained. Some were just plain indifferent. Others were afraid, confused, or disbelieving. Yet others had no excuse at all. The majority of neighbors were elderly, many in their late sixties and seventies. We attributed their passivity to fear. Some retreated from their original statements to the police, omitting details they believed would cause them to be called as witnesses during the trial. Two men living in the Marbury had the gall to claim they'd called the police upon hearing Kitty's screams. Confronted with the police reports of their original statements, they backed down and finally admitted the truth. Other neighbors took the opposite tack, exaggerating their knowledge about the events in hopes of being called as witnesses and basking in their fifteen minutes of fame. We didn't call them as witnesses. Had we done so, no doubt they would have earned themselves fifteen minutes of ridicule instead.

After completing our interviews with the first group of neighbors, we hadn't selected a single one for the witness stand. Would we ever find someone who would help our case?

Late one night, Frank, Jack Peters, and I visited the crime scene. We drove in Cacciatore's car and parked in the bus stop, exactly where Moseley parked before getting out and chasing Kitty. Leaving Peters at the site of the first attack, Frank and I were admitted to the Marbury lobby by prearranged agreement with the superintendent. Both of us sat in the chair that Fink had occupied during the early morning hours of March 13. The chair gave us a clear view of Peters across the street. Not only could we identify his features, but we could also see the blade of the knife he was wielding as he simulated the murder. We decided, after completing our interviews with additional witnesses, that we would have a police department engineer diagram the area, making exact measurements of the distance of any given witness from the attack site.

As luck would have it, Robert Mozer was the first neighbor we spoke to the next morning. An elderly man who lived on the seventh floor of the Marbury, Mozer was pleasant and cooperative. On the night of the attack he'd been sleeping in his bedroom, which fronted Austin Street and was directly across the street from the point where Moseley first caught up to Kitty. Police interviews confirmed that a male voice had yelled out, "What's going on down there? What's going on down there?" After speaking a few minutes to Mozer, we were convinced he was that man. He confirmed some of the details of the first attack that we had learned from Fink and admitted yelling out from his window, though he wasn't one hundred percent sure of his exact words. After yelling, he saw Moseley leaning over Kitty, but as soon as he yelled out, Moseley turned and ran up Austin Street. Mozer was unable to identify him as the attacker, because he never got a full frontal view of Moseley, who, when running away, only provided Mozer with a brief view of his back. Although Mozer wouldn't be the perfect witness, we decided to call him to the stand and let him testify to those details he did recall. He was a credible witness. He admitted to feeling guilty after the fact, but I felt he didn't deserve it. After all, he believed by yelling out that he had stopped whatever it was that was going on outside.

The next person we interviewed was Sophie Farrar, Kitty's next-door neighbor, who had called the police and was the first and only person to rush to her side. We admired and respected her for her reaction that night and decided to call Sophie as a witness despite the fact that her testimony didn't connect Moseley to the attack. By calling her, we could contrast Farrar's and her compassion with Moseley's cold-blooded lack of concern for human life. This, we hoped, would focus jurors' minds on Moseley's crime rather than the neighbors' passivity.

The other neighbors we interviewed offered very little testimony important to establishing Moseley's guilt. Three, however, were able to help us establish the sequence of events on the night of March 13, and we planned to call them as witnesses: Andrée Picq, Samuel Koshkin, and Irene Frost.

The week before the trial began, Cacciatore and I had to prepare for the possible insanity defense. According to New York State law in 1964, a person was legally insane at the time of the commission of a crime if he or she didn't know the nature of the act or understand that it was wrong. Known as the McNaughton Rule and derived from old English case law, it differed from the standard of competency required to put an accused person on trial. The McNaughton Rule didn't refer to psychiatric insanity. A person could be diagnosed as psychologically insane and still be legally sane.

Many of the facts established at the trial from eyewitness testimony or Moseley's confession, or any we might elicit from Moseley on the

witness stand detailing his actions in committing the crime and fleeing, had the potential to defeat an insanity defense. These facts included
Moseley's running away after hearing Mozer yell, moving his car, which
suggested he was trying to hide his license plate, and replacing his stocking cap with a fedora, which implied he was trying to avoid identification.
We also had—or at least thought we had—supporting testimony from
the two forensic psychiatrists at Kings County Hospital who had determined that Moseley was mentally competent to stand trial, Dr. Emil
Winkler and Dr. Jorge Jimenez. As a result, we believed a jury would
reject Moseley's insanity defense and find him guilty.

In addition to tackling a possible insanity defense, we were bent on
extracting from Moseley, in the event he testified, as many details as we
could describing the Kralik homicide for which he claimed responsibility. Those I could use during the Mitchell trial to discredit Moseley's
claim.

In preparing for the trial, we dealt first with the issue of proving Moseley's guilt of murder in the first degree beyond a reasonable
doubt, followed by the testimony we would offer in a post trial hearing to determine whether to impose the death penalty. To this end, we
carefully reviewed the files and police reports of a number of women
who had been raped or sodomized by Moseley or upon whom he had
attempted sexual assaults. These reports supported the argument that
Moseley hadn't killed Barbara Kralik. He was a coward who had never
approached or stalked any woman unless she was obviously alone and
defenseless. Winston Moseley would never break into a house occupied
by anyone other than his intended victim. His modus operandi didn't fit
one detail in the homicide of Barbara Kralik.

That didn't make my job of proving Alvin Mitchell's confession true
and convicting him of Barbara's murder any less difficult. Most members
of the media, the defense bar in Queens, even people in the DA's office,
but above all, the DA himself, Frank O'Connor, still believed that Moseley had killed Kralik. My biggest concern in the Mitchell trial became,
not the possibility that I would be prosecuting the wrong person, but
that Mitchell could get away with killing Barbara Kralik. Judge Shapiro

and Frank O'Connor could afford the luxury of feeling it was fine for me to try a losing case for the experience. I didn't feel the same way. A fifteen-year-old girl was dead as the result of a criminal homicide, and her killer had to answer for it.

One Sunday morning, a few days before the Moseley trial began, I received a phone call from Frank Cacciatore.

"Dr. Winkler's going to change his testimony," he told me ominously. We had worked with Dr. Winkler and gone over his testimony; he had assured us that Moseley knew the nature of his act and understood that it was wrong, in other words, that he was legally sane.

I jumped in my car and drove to Frank's home in Astoria. He was waiting outside, and we left immediately for Winkler's apartment in Sunnyside, Queens.

When we arrived, Mrs. Winkler, who was acquainted with Frank, greeted him warmly. "Herr Doktor is expecting you," she said in her heavy German accent and led us into the living room where Winkler sat with an embarrassed look on his face.

"Is it true you intend to change your testimony?" Frank said.

"Yes," he replied, twisting in his chair. "I'm going to be neutral. I'll testify that I don't know if Moseley knew what he was doing was wrong."

It was the first time I'd ever seen Frank shaken.

We spent the next hour trying to learn why he'd changed his mind and impressing upon him and his wife the viciousness of Moseley's crime. It was all to no avail. The doctor wouldn't tell us the reason for his decision, and we couldn't change his mind. Cacciatore later told me he had heard rumors that Sidney Sparrow, Moseley's lead attorney, had influenced Dr. Winkler's opinion but never learned how or any details.

We left, disappointed and in a quandary. With only a few days left before a trial that Judge Shapiro would surely never delay, it was too late for further psychiatric testing. As a last resort, we decided to contact an independent psychiatrist to review all of Moseley's psychiatric records and observe him in court. Based on what he read and saw, the psychiatrist would render an opinion of the defendant's sanity.

That afternoon we contacted Dr. Frank Cassino, chief of psychiatry at Wyckoff Heights Hospital, who agreed to meet with us the following morning. Our discussions of the insanity defense were based on the practical application of the governing statute, which didn't once mention medical or psychiatric insanity. Moseley had originally been diagnosed by Dr. Winkler and Dr. Jimenez as suffering from periodic catatonic schizophrenia, which meant complete withdrawal from contact with people. But that technical interpretation wasn't the issue. The issue was much more basic: did the defendant know he was killing Kitty, and did he know it was wrong to kill her? In considering an insanity defense, these were the two questions the jury would have to ponder.

Our preparation concentrated on evidence that affirmatively answered the "know" questions. We meticulously prepared a number of questions for Moseley's cross-examination that would induce him to use his own words that would destroy what was the only defense on which he could realistically rely.

One issue we had to confront involved the sentence hearing on the death penalty should Moseley be convicted. Would the defense attorneys be permitted to offer Moseley's mental condition in evidence for a jury to consider mitigating the death sentence? And should we object to such testimony? If Judge Shapiro were to agree with our opposition to admitting such evidence and the jury were to decide in favor of the death penalty, an appellate court could set the penalty aside and substitute its judgment for that of the jury. We agreed that this was a decision for the Chief to make. Cacciatore called O'Connor, and he directed us to object to such testimony. He didn't have a problem with the appellate court being the final arbiter of such an issue. "That's what they're there for," he said.

We met with Dr. Cassino the following morning and gave him all the psychiatric records we had of Moseley as well as his confessions. After detailing Moseley's actions on the night of the murder, we left the doctor alone to ponder the issue of Moseley's legal insanity.

We met later that evening. "It would be helpful if I could watch Moseley in court and listen to his testimony," he said. "But from everything I've read so far, I'm confident that on the night of March 13, Moseley knew that he was killing a human being and knew that it was wrong. I'll testify to that at the trial."

In preparing for the possible death penalty hearing, we selected a group of six women from the files we had studied to use as possible witnesses and interviewed them the Saturday before the trial. One was Annie Mae Johnson's neighbor, who would testify about that homicide. Four women had all been assaulted by Moseley with either a gun or a knife. He had committed acts of sodomy and rape against two of the women, two others had barely escaped before he had a chance to complete his crime, and the fifth, unlike Kitty, managed to outrun Moseley before he had a chance to harm her. We decided to have all six available at the end of the trial, in the event Judge Shapiro permitted us to call them as witnesses.

At last, our preparation was over. We were as ready as circumstances allowed us to be for the trial of Winston Moseley.

CHAPTER SEVEN

The criminal court building was located two city blocks east of where Kitty Genovese was brutally slain. When I arrived at the DA's wing at about 7:30 a.m. on June 8, 1964, a large crowd was already milling around in the courthouse lobby. The New York press had spread the word that jury selection was starting today, and as I elbowed my way through the pack of court buffs, rubbernecking retirees, curiosity seekers, and voracious consumers of tabloid news, I could just imagine what it would be like when the trial proper started—a circus.

I met Frank in his office, and we reviewed our notes, not that it was necessary—we just needed to get past our pretrial jitters.

At about 9:15 we wheeled our shopping cart of files to Judge Shapiro's courtroom on the third floor of the new courthouse. Bedlam had broken out in the hallway. Hundreds of men and women of every description jammed the floor, all vying for entry. The crowd spilled down the stairs to the large vestibule and onto the sidewalks outside. Earlier, a court officer had informed the crowd by loudspeaker that only a limited number of spectators would be permitted to see the trial. The courtroom was relatively small, with two sections of approximately twelve rows of benches that accommodated no more than one hundred, and the press would have priority. Obviously, the officer's remarks hadn't deterred a soul.

Judge Shapiro, known for his punctuality and obsession with moving cases along without delay, entered his elegant, redwood-paneled court-room at precisely 9:30. We hoped he wouldn't rush the process of jury selection, since we wanted to make sure no person was selected who had conscientious scruples against the death penalty. As for the trial, if it were to be rushed, the prosecution would suffer, not the defense. Frank and I needed the cruel details of Moseley's crimes to sink in, to be embedded in jurors' minds and not passed over quickly. It was those details that would help us overcome an insanity defense and possibly put Moseley on death row.

As we'd expected, before sending for the panel of prospective jurors, the judge permitted Moseley's lead defense counsel, Sidney Sparrow, to add the defense of insanity.

Realizing the difficulty of assembling an impartial jury after the media blitz surrounding the Genovese case, Shapiro had seen to it that the panel of prospective jurors was enlarged. Ignoring the crowd outside his door, Shapiro ordered the courtroom locked during jury selection. The jury panel took up every available seat in the courtroom, and no media representatives or spectators were permitted inside.

Judge Shapiro took over most of the questioning of prospective jurors. It was the usual practice in federal court for a judge to do such questioning, but few judges adopted the practice in the New York State Supreme Court, Shapiro being the lone exception in Queens. Much to our relief, Shapiro didn't rush the job. He exercised great pains to be certain the jurors hadn't made up their minds about Moseley's guilt or innocence. In his wisdom, he was ensuring that in the event of an appeal, no one could argue that jury selection hadn't been fair. Furthermore, he brilliantly covered any problems of possible prejudice arising from the collective guilt of Queens's residents resulting from the failure of Kitty's neighbors to come to her aid.

When Frank and I questioned the jurors, we limited our questioning to whether any had conscientious scruples about the death penalty. One juror said, "I did have scruples against the death penalty when I filled out the county clerk form several years ago, but I've since changed my mind." When it came time to decide whether to excuse this juror, both Frank and I agreed to retain him on the theory that nobody is more fanatical than a convert.

Sidney Sparrow was an outstanding criminal defense attorney with a unique talent; he had spent many hours in court, producing lifelike sketches while waiting for his cases to be called. Articulate and analytical, capable of breaking down the most complicated case so that a jury could easily grasp the issues, he was respected by all the assistant DAs, and O'Connor as well.

Sparrow and his defense team did just what I expected—they spent a great deal of time trying to maximize the effect of the neighbors' passivity on the conscience of the prospective jurors. No doubt the attorneys hoped that by harping on the neighbors, they could shift to them some of the universal animosity in Queens toward Moseley and perhaps avoid the death penalty.

The jury that resulted consisted of twelve men and several alternates. No women were chosen from the few on the panel (at that time women weren't called for jury duty, though they could serve on a voluntary basis). Aside from that fact, the jury was a cross section of the Queens populace, and both prosecution and defense were satisfied with the selection.

After calling a recess, Judge Shapiro ordered the courtroom opened to the press and spectators and then withdrew to his chambers. A mad dash for seats ensued, with plenty of pushing and shoving, and at one point a fistfight almost broke out. When he returned to the courtroom, Shapiro announced that in the future only ten spectators would be permitted to enter the courtroom at a time until it was filled, and no one would be permitted to leave or enter while the trial was in progress.

The trial commenced with the prosecution's opening statement. Cacciatore rose from his chair and strode over to the jury box. Before saying a word, he looked directly into the eyes of each juror. Then, slowly and stopping frequently to lock eyes with the jurors, he read the indictment charging murder in the first degree. Without using any notes, he presented a capsule description of Winston Moseley's violent attacks on Kitty.

"The People will show that after 3:00 a.m., and possibly 3:15, 3:20, screams were heard by many people...'Help me, help me I'm being stabbed,' or words to that effect."

Then he summarized Moseley's description to the detectives of his second attack on Kitty in the vestibule: "He told them that as he saw her lying on the floor moaning, she looked up at him, and as she saw him, she started to scream, and so he stabbed her, and he told them where—in the throat, where the noise was coming from, where the screaming was coming from..."

His opening statement included testimony from the neighbors we planned to use as witnesses. Frank gave special emphasis to the anticipated testimony of Sophie Farrar, who he said "saw Kitty fully exposed."

So that the jurors wouldn't shift their fury from Moseley to Kitty's neighbors, Frank deliberately left out any mention of their failure to come to her aid.

It was obvious that Frank's opening was having the effect on the jurors that we were hoping for. With each new brutal detail, they seemed to shift their eyes from Frank and glared—at least that's how I saw it—at Moseley seated at the defense table surrounded by his attorneys.

When it was time for Sidney Sparrow's opening statement, he rose almost grimacing, attempting a plea for sympathy, and slowly made his way to the jury box. Sparrow's opening statement was considerably longer than Frank's, but failing to support each detail with testimony would be damaging to the defense. Right away, it became clear that the defense would rely solely on the plea that Moseley was legally insane at the time he attacked Kitty. It didn't surprise me. After all, it was the only possible defense for someone who had so openly confessed to the murder by providing details only the killer would know.

Sparrow presented a long history of his client, beginning from his childhood. Moseley's parents had an on and off again relationship. Once, after they separated, Sparrow said, "He became a pawn between mother and father and...there were continuous quarrels and problems concerning the infidelity of his mother, who had run off to live with another man..." He lived with his father and an aunt, and "when he reached the age of seventeen, a friend of this aunt, also a Negress, initiated him into the concepts of sex. She was a married woman too, just as his mother had been when she left his father for another man." Sparrow claimed it was this background, in addition to other family problems that had helped foster in Moseley a hatred of women, especially full-breasted blacks. Sparrow openly admitted that his client had committed many burglaries, as well as sexual attacks and other brutal acts against women, including, he claimed, Annie Mae Johnson and Barbara Kralik. He provided the details of each murder to which Sparrow claimed his client would testify.

When Sparrow finished his opening statement, Judge Shapiro recessed the trial until the following morning. Leaving the courtroom, Frank and I had to shove our way past the horde of reporters and spectators peppering us with questions. Propelling ourselves forward was enough of a feat; the task was made more difficult because of our shopping cart. We had to guard it carefully, as it contained, in addition to our files, the hunting knife with which Moseley had slain his victim; police photographs taken in the early morning hours of March 13; schematic drawings; Kitty's wallet, which was recovered in the bushes across the street from Moseley's place of employment; and his original signed confession.

"How many neighbors are you going to call during the trial?" That was the most pressing question on reporters' minds. We remained silent and continued pushing on until we'd covered the hundred yards that separated the courtroom from the DA's wing. Closing the door behind me, I leaned against it and breathed a sigh of relief.

Back in Frank's office, we discussed whether or not to alter our plans in light of Sparrow's approach, openly admitting that his client had committed the crime for which he was on trial. We agreed to stick with our plan as prepared and with the witnesses we'd lined up.

The following morning, after running the spectator gauntlet once again, we entered the courtroom to begin our prosecution case. I scanned the spectators' seats, hoping against hope to find someone in Kitty's immediate family present. It would help our case to have at least one relative with whom the jury could relate. But it wasn't to be—no one showed. During our trial preparation with Vito Genovese, Kitty's uncle, (no relation to the crime boss) who had identified her body as required by law in a murder trial, we had learned not to anticipate any cooperation from Kitty's immediate family, her parents, or her three brothers and sister. He told us the family had suffered greatly from their loss. Together with the notoriety, the family didn't want to appear in court and subject themselves to an onslaught from the press.

The first witness we called was Victor Horan, the bartender who had worked with Kitty in Ev's 11th Hour, to establish the time she left the bar to drive home. The next to appear was police engineer Lieutenant John Cashman, who had prepared the schematics indicating how far each witness to the crime had been from the scene.

Our next four witnesses were ones the public especially wanted to hear from: Kitty's four neighbors—Robert Mozer, Andrée Picq, Irene Frost, and Samuel Koshkin—a representative cross section of Kew Gardens. Collectively, they reconstructed the sequence of events on the night of March 13, starting with Kitty's screams for help, Moseley returning to his parked car and changing headgear, his search for Kitty, and the final attack. During key moments of testimony, Winston Moseley sat still as a statue at the defense counsel table. In reaction to the parade of witnesses, he never appeared to move a muscle or blink an eye.

Their testimony was a prosecutor's dream. It went exactly as we'd hoped, and we didn't waste time focusing on their passivity in the face of horror. Although we had anticipated these witnesses would be uneasy, because they realized there could be some hostility toward them, they delivered their testimony without displaying fear, hesitation, or nervousness.

The testimony of Edward Feisler, the milkman who had seen Moseley leaving the scene after the second attack, was equally helpful, for he was able to identify him.

The next witness up was Sophie Farrar. She entered the courtroom a split second after Frank called out her name, dressed in a simple suit and looking tinier than I'd remembered. It was the first time her identity was revealed—she had never been interviewed by anyone other than detectives, myself, or Frank—and as she advanced up the center aisle, the journalists were feverishly scribbling in their steno pads. She glanced contemptuously at Moseley before turning toward the raised witness chair that faced the prosecution table. Despite her petite stature, she looked confident, which didn't surprise me. I knew she was anxious to testify, for she had been genuinely fond of Kitty.

The courtroom was silent during Sophie's testimony, jurors and spectators alike hanging on her every word. Describing what she saw when entering the vestibule, Sophie testified, "I saw Kitty laying down; she was stretched out in the hall...Her head was towards the door...and her clothes were all torn, or ripped; I don't know what it was; and she was all exposed...top and bottom...she was just moaning. I was talking to her." Sophie didn't notice any blood "until I held her hand and I had blood all over my hands. And then she moved, and I saw all the blood from under her back, and then I noticed she had holes in her coat."

After identifying the police photographs of the vestibule, Sophie left the witness chair without being questioned by Sparrow. As she exited the courtroom, I could see the jurors following her every step with admiration as if to say, at least someone had displayed courage in Kew Gardens on March 13.

Our next witness was Mary Ann Zielonko, Kitty's roommate and co manager of the bar. Although Frank and I knew Mary Ann and Kitty had been lovers, we had never disclosed the nature of their relationship and neither had any detective. Lesbian relationships weren't generally accepted in those days, and we didn't want theirs to jeopardize the outcome of the trial. One could not help staring admiringly at Mary Ann as she took the stand. With her short blonde hair, she was stunningly beautiful, bearing a remarkable resemblance to Hollywood icon Kim Novak. Her testimony was brief; limited only to identifying the wallet of Kitty's that detectives had recovered adjacent to Moseley's place of employment.

Sidney Sparrow and the other defense attorneys didn't ask a single question of any of these witnesses, conceding all of their testimony. In view of Sparrow's opening statement, in which he openly admitted that

Moseley killed Kitty, Frank and I were not surprised. However, we had expected the defense attorney, at the very least, to question Mozer, Picq, Frost, and Koshkin in order to highlight Kitty's neighbors' passivity during the attacks.

All that remained for us to do was introduce into evidence Moseley's signed confession, his oral admissions to Lieutenant Bernard Jacobs and the other police officers, and Vito Genovese's identification of Kitty's body.

Other than the police witnesses, we called only one more witness to the stand: Dr. William Benenson, the medical examiner who had performed Kitty's autopsy.

When Frank asked him about the cause of death, Benenson testified, "The essential facts were that she had multiple stab wounds scattered over the various parts of the body, that two of these stab wounds had penetrated the right and left chest releasing air into the chest cavity."

Frank questioned Benenson about something we had anticipated Sparrow would emphasize during the defense case—the alleged wounds to Kitty's vaginal area. In confession, Moseley had claimed to have inserted his knife there.

"Doctor," Frank said, "did you examine the vaginal area of the deceased, Kitty Genovese?"

"Yes, I did. There was no evidence of any recent injury, no positive evidence of there having been any sexual assault."

Sparrow took a risk in his cross-examination, questioning Dr. Benenson in detail about all of the knife wounds he observed during the autopsy. Sparrow's purpose was clearly to plant in jurors' minds the belief that only a psychopath could commit such a brutal crime. Not one juror was able to look or even glance in Moseley's direction, but that didn't mean they would let Moseley off the hook on an insanity defense. In fact, it suggested that they wouldn't.

We had deliberately kept our presentation of the prosecution case relatively brief, so as not to muddy the waters; we wanted to leave no doubt that Moseley was Kitty's killer, that he was viciously brutal, and that he was in command of his faculties when he committed the crime.

We anticipated the insanity defense by repeating Moseley's rational, detailed descriptions of the crime to Lieutenant Jacobs and Assistant DA Chetta.

Picking up Moseley's signed confession, Cacciatore faced the jurors as he read it. I tried to read the jurors' reaction. During Dr. Benenson's testimony they couldn't even look at the defendant; this time, they glanced repeatedly at him.

"She got out of the car," Frank read, "and she saw me, and she was frightened right away, and she started to run. I ran after her and stabbed her twice in the back. Somebody yelled, and I was frightened. So I jumped back into the car, backed the car back to the nearest cross street and backed down this street about half a block…I noticed as I was backing the car back that the woman had gotten up and appeared to be going around the corner. So I came back thinking that I would find her. The second door I tried opened, and there she was laying on the floor. When she saw me, she started screaming again. So I stabbed her a few more times. She seemed to quiet down a little bit. So she wasn't really struggling that hard with me now. So I lifted up her skirt, and I cut off her girdle. I even cut or pulled her panties off, and she had a sanitary pad, and I picked that out and threw it away, and I stabbed her again in the stomach. I cut off her brassiere, and I don't remember whether I cut her blouse or not, and I took one of the false pads that she had in the brassiere, because it had blood on it, and I touched it with my finger, and I didn't want to leave it. I attempted to have sexual intercourse with her, but I was unable to as I was impotent. I did have an orgasm, however…"

When he'd finished reading, Frank rested the prosecution case in time for the lunch recess.

The defense began its case in the afternoon with the testimony orchestrated to lay a foundation for the insanity defense. Fannie Moseley, the defendant's mother, testified that Alphonse Moseley, her husband, was not the biological father of the defendant, a fact withheld from him until late in his childhood. Nevertheless, the defendant had always considered Alphonse his father and continued to live with him and an aunt after

Fannie and Alphonse separated. Thereafter she saw the defendant five or six times a year while he was growing up. After testifying that she had had the surgical removal of a stomach tumor—obviously designed to show the defendant's insane abhorrence and brutalization of the internal organs of women—she testified to the defendant's love for dogs and his children. Fannie was then turned over to Cacciatore for cross-examination. It was brief but notable for the interruption by Judge Shapiro, who pointedly questioned the witness about the time she lived with the defendant and his second wife, Elizabeth.

"Tell me, madam, the four years you lived in the house…you had frequent conversations with the defendant, and you heard him engage in conversations with his wife?" Shapiro asked.

"Yes, sir."

"Did you have any trouble understanding him?"

"No."

"He was quite coherent at all times, wasn't he?"

"Yes."

The next defense witness was Alphonse Moseley. After stating that he had lived off and on again with Fannie and she had left him at times for another man, Alphonse went on to testify about the defendant's interests in mice, snakes, chipmunks, but especially ants, for which he had built the defendant his first aquarium in his early years.

This testimony was offered to further prove the defendant's irrational interest in and concern for insects and animals as opposed to his complete disregard of the value of a human life, of course with the exception of his immediate family.

Frank's cross-examination was limited to the various items Winston Moseley had brought to Alphonse's store, such as television sets and the like, which the witness claimed he didn't know were stolen.

The next defense witness was the defendant's first wife, Pauline, who said she had married Moseley when she was seventeen and he was nineteen. Married in February, they had their first child in July and a second child almost two years later. A year later, "I got involved with another man," she testified. This resulted in divorce. Like Alphonse, Pauline testified to the defendant's fascination with ants, describing how he would dig them up, put them in a cage and feed them sugar, bread crumbs, and live roaches.

Frank didn't cross-examine Pauline, and Sparrow next called Elizabeth Moseley, the defendant's second and current wife. An attractive black woman, she was articulate and obviously intelligent. A registered nurse employed at City Hospital in Elmhurst, Queens, she had married the defendant in 1961 and had their only child almost two years later. Much to my surprise, her testimony was brief, much shorter than the previous defense witness. Like the others before her, she described her husband's fascination with ants. Testifying to details about the couple's sexual practices, she said they were normal. Apparently, Elizabeth had no inkling of her husband's rapacious nighttime activities. She worked nights, he days, and he was always home when she called at 7:00 a.m. to wake him to go to work. Elizabeth's testimony didn't disclose the nature of her husband's relationship with or feelings toward the children.

If Elizabeth's cross-examination was uneventful, the next promised to be the opposite.

"Call your next witness," Judge Shapiro directed Sparrow.

"Winston Moseley."

There was a noticeable buzz in the courtroom followed by complete silence. All eyes, except the jurors, turned toward the defense table as the defendant rose and approached the witness chair. Moseley was a light skinned, slightly built black man. He didn't appear to be the least bit nervous. Dressed in a sport jacket, slacks, shirt, and tie, he maintained the stoic stance he had adopted from the beginning, never betraying any emotion. The only sounds now were the muted clicking of his shoes against the tile floor and the faint scratching as reporters feverishly jotted notes in their stenographic pads. Passing the prosecution table where Frank and I were seated, the defendant looked straight ahead as if we were invisible.

Under Sparrow's unusually soft questioning, Moseley testified to his unstable childhood—the constant bickering between his parents, his mother leaving the family a number of times, and his living with

Alphonse, even after he learned that Alphonse was not his biological father. His testimony was clearly intended to convey such an abnormal childhood and upbringing that it had to result in a severe psychosis.

Much to my chagrin, before Judge Shapiro recessed the trial until the following day, Sparrow brought up the Barbara Kralik case, asking Moseley a couple of questions about it. "Were you in Springfield Gardens on July 20, 1963?" and "Did you kill Barbara Kralik?" Without hesitation, the defendant answered yes.

I didn't want the subject to come up at this point in Moseley's testimony. I knew the press would emphasize the dual confessions before we had a chance to cross-examine him and bring out any inconsistencies. The press was hostile enough, and we didn't need to end a day with statements damaging to the Mitchell prosecution.

The following morning was the typical mob scene. Jack Peters and another detective had to open a path through the crowd so that Frank and I could gain access to the courtroom. Later, when the courtroom doors were unlocked, there was bedlam as spectators and journalists rushed to find seats, elbowing and pushing each other to get close to the witness chair.

Sparrow continued his questioning related to Barbara Kralik. Moseley described taking a small steak knife from his home on the night of July 19 and picking the Kralik house at about 3:00 a.m. on July 20, because "it had a window, which I thought would be easy for me to get into…"

He said he had "never been there before and didn't know any of the occupants of the house." He then continued, "So I went upstairs, and when I got up there, I could see there were two people asleep in one room, which I imagine were a mother and a father, and there was somebody asleep in the other room…The other person appeared to be a young girl to me, and I looked at her for maybe a few seconds, and then I took the knife that I had and stabbed her to death, and as I was stabbing her, she squirmed. I had my hand over her mouth. She made some sort of sound, and whoever was in the other room called out to her. When they called out to her, I turned around and walked away. I walked out of the house and out of the side door, which I had opened before I came upstairs."

This was the first time I learned any details from Moseley about his claim of killing Barbara Kralik, and it was more than disturbing. Could some of the details have been learned from the newspaper articles written about the Kralik homicide or from other sources? I was certain I would never discover the answer to that question. Moseley wouldn't admit it—nor would anyone else who might have fed him the details. But one thing was clear—his testifying to killing Barbara in such detail could make it nearly impossible for me to convict the person I believed was the real killer, Alvin Mitchell.

Next, Sparrow elicited from Moseley the details of how he had killed Annie Mae Johnson. He testified that he had shot her to death, then disrobed her and attempted intercourse even though he believed her to be dead. He described how he dragged her body into her house and set it afire by placing a burning scarf to her genitals. No mention was made of the botched autopsy.

None of these gory details could break his granite facade. With chilling impassivity, he reviewed the choreography of his most notorious crime, the murder of Kitty Genovese, delivering his comments in a monotone voice: "Well, I left the house at about 1:30 or 2 o'clock, and it took me until about 3 o'clock to find one that was driving where I could actually catch up with her, and so I did see this car about 3 o'clock, a red car, and I followed it for about ten blocks. And then it pulled into what I thought was just a parking lot next to a building, and I parked in a bus stop that was as close as I could park to the car…

"As soon as she got out of the car, she saw me and she ran. I ran after her, and I had a knife in my hand then, and I caught up with her, and I stabbed her twice in the back, and somebody did call out of the window, and when they called out of the window, then I realized that I had parked my car probably where they could have seen it, so I went back…and…when I was backing the car away, I could see that she had gotten up and she wasn't dead.

"I didn't go home, because I didn't think that the person that called would come down to help her regardless of the fact that she had screamed...I could see that she had walked around the building the other way from when she started running...The second door was open, and she was in there. As soon as she saw me, she started screaming so I stabbed her a few other times to stop her from screaming, and I had stabbed her once in the neck, yes. When I stabbed her in the neck, she only moaned after that...

"Well, after she stopped struggling...I could hear there were people awake upstairs...I heard the door open up there at least twice, maybe three times, but when I looked...there was nobody up there, and I didn't feel that these people were coming down the stairs anyway, so after she wasn't struggling with me anymore, I lifted up her skirt and did cut off her underclothes, and I pulled up her blouse or cut it—I'm not sure which—and cut off her brassiere."

Not a sound could be heard in the courtroom other than Moseley's words. The reporters had stopped writing in their pads, and some of the jurors sat with their jaws dropped, as if in disbelief.

Hearing this last bit of Moseley's testimony, I realized that Frank and I had done the right thing in not calling Karl Ross to the witness stand, the man who had opened the door at the top of the staircase during the second attack. The jurors might consider his inaction as a contributing factor in Kitty's death, possibly enough to compromise the death penalty. They were bound to believe as Frank and I did that Ross was lying when he told the police that he hadn't seen anything during Moseley's vicious second attack. Again, we didn't want to distract jurors from the real issue, Moseley's crime.

On cross-examination of Moseley, Frank managed to elicit from Moseley the admission that he had denied Barbara Kralik's killing to Dr. Winkler and Dr. Jimenez when he was examined for his capacity to stand trial. Furthermore, Moseley testified that there were only two bedrooms upstairs in the Kralik house and that only two adults and Barbara were upstairs. In fact, there were three bedrooms upstairs and three adults—the grandmother included—not just two.

Moseley's testimony, both direct and on cross-examination, revealed him to be a person without remorse or compassion for his victims or their families. It was clear that he had not given even a moment of thought to the havoc he had wreaked. While delivering his harrowing account of multiple murders, the only sympathy he harbored was for Winston Moseley. When Cacciatore asked, "Did you feel sorry for the victims?" Moseley replied, "No, I don't."

So, was he legally crazy? Did he know what he was doing? Did he know that the acts he committed were wrong?

Two psychiatrists were produced by the defense, Dr. Oscar Diamond and Dr. Emil Winkler. Dr. Diamond was director of the Manhattan State Hospital and a clinical professor of psychiatry at several medical schools. He testified that while Moseley did know the nature and quality of his acts, he was suffering from such a defect in reasoning that he didn't know his acts were wrong. Diamond described him as suffering from schizophrenia characterized by paranoid delusions. The defendant's aberrant actions involving the genitalia and the supposed fact that he had shot Annie Mae Johnson and stabbed Kitty Genovese, the doctor testified, supported the opinion that Moseley had a marked hostility toward women.

Cacciatore was unable to shake Dr. Diamond's opinion on cross-examination.

Next, Sparrow called Dr. Winkler, the chief of psychiatry at Kings County Hospital, who had told Cacciatore and me that he would support the defense claim of insanity. Like Dr. Diamond, Winkler testified that Moseley knew the nature and quality of his act. However, when asked if Moseley knew it was wrong, Winkler qualified his opinion by saying that Moseley's "knowledge of what is right and wrong was severely impaired."

Their testimony ended the defense case, and we followed it by calling Dr. Cassino as a rebuttal witness. A psychiatrist with impeccable credentials, Cassino stated emphatically that on March 13, 1964, Moseley knew the nature and quality of his act and was able to distinguish between right and wrong.

Before the trial had begun, Judge Shapiro indicated his intention to keep the proceedings moving along without delay. He ran a tight ship. On June 10, after only three days of testimony, court was recessed. The next day, closing arguments would begin.

With each passing day, the crowds in the corridor seemed to grow larger. The regular court buffs knew summations would take place on the eleventh, and that morning the crowd was packed so tightly it actually took Frank, Jack, and me almost twenty minutes to push our way through the fifty yards from the elevator to the courtroom door. As we slowly made our way, reporters were throwing questions at us without even waiting for answers. "How's it going?" "Do you think the neighbors hurt your case?" "Will the jury get the case today?" "Will you push for the death penalty if he is convicted?" We ignored their questions and plowed on. Later I was told that by the time of the closing arguments, hundreds of spectators spilled outside the courthouse onto Queens Boulevard.

In his closing statement, Sidney Sparrow drove home his contention that the defendant hadn't been aware of doing anything wrong in killing Kitty. He rehashed every detail of his client's murderous attacks on Annie Mae Johnson and Kitty Genovese, and he worked the Barbara Kralik case into his argument as if part of his confession were true. As Sparrow described the Kralik killing, I could see the reporters absorbing his remarks while writing in their steno pads. Sparrow was relying on the commonly used argument in a murder case with an insanity defense: only a person with a diseased mind who didn't know right from wrong could have committed crimes in this manner against individuals he didn't know. However, Sparrow went too far when he stated that the burden of proof for an insanity defense was on the people. Judge Shapiro immediately interrupted.

"That is not the law," he said. "I will not so charge. The People do not have any burden of proving that the defendant is sane."

In the end, Sparrow pleaded with the jurors to "walk humbly with God."

Frank Cacciatore's closing statement, which we had prepared as a kickoff for the hearing on the death penalty, dwelled on the brutal nature of Moseley's attacks and his lack of compassion for the pain and suffering inflicted on his victims. As for the insanity issue, his attack against the defense psychiatrists was a common sense approach. The defense doctors based their opinion solely on the subjective statements made to them by the defendant and his relatives, all of whom knew that insanity was his only defense. Neither doctor made the slightest attempt to verify what he was being told. Why should they be believed?

Judge Shapiro's charge to the jury was comprehensive. He reviewed the testimony of all the witnesses, including those who had weighed in on legal insanity, then directed the jury to commence deliberations. His instructions on the law had been meticulously prepared, leaving no room for the defendant to argue on appeal that the court had made a serious legal mistake.

After only six hours, the jurors filed back into the courtroom to deliver their verdict. When the first juror emerged, a murmur went up among the spectators, and the courtroom grew as quiet as Shea Stadium is when the bases are loaded and the ball is sailing toward the plate. The jurors stared straight ahead as they filed into the jury box.

The court clerk asked, "Madam and gentlemen of the jury, have you agreed upon a verdict?"

The foreman, Irving I. Helfman, answered without hesitation, "We the jury find the defendant, Winston Moseley, guilty as charged."

With these words, a loud cheer erupted in the courtroom from the spectators. I could see Shapiro squirming, about to gavel them into silence. Before he did, someone opened the door to the courtroom, and we could hear a roar of approval emanate from the hallway and outside on Queens Boulevard. The people were ecstatic.

There was no reaction from Moseley when the foreman announced the verdict. He remained as impassive as a block of stone.

Judge Shapiro lost no time scheduling the death penalty hearing for June 15, informing all attorneys that he would brook no delay. He then summoned me and Herbert Lyon, Alvin Mitchell's attorney, to the bench, telling us that the Mitchell trial would commence shortly after the Moseley death penalty hearing, which I knew would last only a few days at most. It would leave me precious little time to complete preparation of the Mitchell trial.

"Go ahead with the Mitchell case," Frank told me. "I can take care of Moseley's penalty phase on my own."

Realistically, there was only one issue to determine at Moseley's penalty hearing: whether his mental condition would mitigate the death penalty. As it turned out, Judge Shapiro didn't even permit evidence of mental illness to be introduced in mitigation of a death sentence. He ruled that the jury, in determining his guilt, had already rejected the insanity defense. Now only one obstacle remained to the imposition of the death penalty, and that was the possibility that one of the jurors had some sort of conscientious objection to such a penalty. The defense could only hope that the jury would transfer some of the guilt for Kitty's death to the neighbors and leave enough room for sympathy for Moseley.

On Monday, June 15, while I was in my office preparing for the Mitchell trial, the jury briefly heard the testimony of four women who had been victimized by Moseley, the four Frank and I had prepared to testify. This was followed by a brief plea in which Sidney Sparrow asked the jury not to impose the death penalty. After hearing their instructions from Judge Shapiro, the jury left the courtroom. It took them only thirty-five minutes to come to a decision. At noon I received a phone call from Frank and rushed to the courtroom to hear the verdict. Elbowing my way through the bodies in the corridor, I glanced out of a window and saw that a huge crowd had gathered on Queens Boulevard below, later estimated to be in the thousands, in anticipation of the jury's decision.

At 12:15, after only fifty minutes of deliberations, the jurors filed in one more time, and from the stern looks on their faces and the way they again avoided eye contact with Moseley, I predicted their verdict. As soon as the jurors had taken their seats, the court clerk asked their decision.

One more time the jury foreman stood up. "We, the jury, prescribe the death penalty for Winston Moseley."

Immediately, the spectators erupted into cheers and applause, and Judge Shapiro threatened to hold anyone in contempt who continued to demonstrate. Moments later, for the second time, a chain reaction of cheers could be heard coming from outside the courtroom and the street below.

Judge Shapiro fixed the sentencing for June 22, one week later. "The sooner we get him out of Queens County and into the death cell, the better," he explained. "Maybe it will act as a deterrent for others, though I don't believe in the deterrent provision myself."

Winston Moseley, the brutal serial criminal, had been tried and convicted in five and a half short days. There was no room in any juror's mind for either sympathy or conscientious objection to the death penalty. After Judge Shapiro discharged the jury, Frank and I spoke to several of them. Each indicated that the failure of Kitty's neighbors to call the police never entered their minds during deliberations. The subject was never discussed.

Though the outcome was what Frank and I had wished for Moseley, any hope I'd harbored that his trial would provide conclusive evidence to help in the prosecution of Alvin Mitchell had vanished. Because Kitty Genovese and Barbara Kralik were white, despite Moseley's admission that all of his sexual crimes were intended to be committed solely against black victims, clearly many people in and out of the justice system, especially the media, still believed that Moseley was Barbara's killer. It was up to me to prove to a jury that he wasn't.

CHAPTER EIGHT

Later that day, Frank, Bernard Patten, and I met with the Chief in his office. "We still have to decide whether to proceed with the Mitchell case," O'Connor said. "I want your thoughts and opinions."

After Patten and Cacciatore argued that all the evidence pointed to Mitchell's guilt, O'Connor turned to me. "Charlie, you've prepared the case and investigated it, you're probably in the best position to offer an opinion."

"I have no doubt that Mitchell killed the Kralik girl, Chief. I've compared the statements and confessions of Borges and Mitchell so thoroughly that I can almost recite them from memory. No police officer could coerce two boys to come up with stories as similar as these are in so many details. I understand that Moseley threw a monkey wrench into the case, but that doesn't mean we should walk away from prosecuting a person we believe killed a fifteen-year-old girl. I'm ready to start the trial. Sure, I wish I had more time to prepare, but that's the way it is."

"Okay, go ahead with the trial," O'Connor said. "Let's see if you can get any jurors to agree with you. If Moseley testifies that he did it, I doubt you'll get a conviction, but do your best."

After the meeting, Cacciatore and I agreed that he wouldn't sit at the prosecution table with me, because he needed to devote the time to his duties as chief of the trial bureau. In the event Moseley testified, however, Frank would handle the cross-examination. Although my detective, Jack Peters, would join me at the table, I would be on my own.

"Try it with what you have, and do the best you can," Frank advised me. "A hung jury will be a victory for the office and the police department, and you only need one juror for a hung jury. Try it for that one juror."

"That would be a role reversal," I remarked sarcastically. Usually a defense attorney tried a case for one juror, since a hung jury was considered a victory for the defense, not the prosecution. The prosecution needed twelve jurors to convict, and the defense needed only one juror to prevent a conviction. "Look, I have no doubt that Mitchell killed Barbara," I went on. "In the event of a hung jury, will you support any efforts I make to convince O'Connor to retry Mitchell and not dismiss the case outright?"

Frank agreed and promised to enlist Patten's aid as well.

Jack Peters and I lost no time. Right away we started lining up witnesses for the trial, knowing that Judge Shapiro would want them called to the stand in quick sequence with no delays. Shapiro's fast processing of the Moseley trial unnerved me. Perhaps the notoriety of the Mitchell case and the heavy media coverage would rein in his well-known impatience.

Late that evening, back at home, I read over some of the newspaper articles published at the time of Mitchell's arrest. I hadn't seen all of the articles during trial preparation, and I thought perhaps now I'd stumble across something that could be of value during the trial.

One article, in the *Long Island Press*, referred to a statement Mitchell had made to a reporter outside police headquarters in Manhattan shortly after his arrest and booking. I phoned Jack and asked him to check with several television networks to see if they had anything on film. The following afternoon, Jack showed up in my office with film from ABC-TV that contained an interview of Alvin Mitchell by TV reporter Jim Burnes.

I locked my office door and turned off the lights. Then Jack and

I watched the interview on a large screen. It was so startling that we replayed it several times. There was Mitchell, appearing unusually relaxed, as if he had just gotten the weight of the world off his shoulders, without a single mark on his face or the slightest appearance of having been in a struggle with police detectives. He was obviously aware of his surroundings, calmly admitting the attack on Barbara Kralik and claiming he had panicked. "I wanted to tell the police from the beginning, but I was scared," he admitted.

What a bombshell! I thought. It would be invaluable in answering two questions: Were Mitchell's confessions voluntary? And were his other statements to the police and Assistant DA Stanley Pryor truthful? While this newly discovered film didn't eliminate the possibility of a jury finding reasonable doubt about Mitchell's guilt arising from Moseley's confession, it would make jurors think seriously before voting to acquit. Perhaps it would find me the one juror Frank Cacciatore thought I should be looking for to hang the jury.

Later that day I replayed the film for Cacciatore, O'Connor, and Patten. All three were stunned. After viewing it, the Chief motioned for me to stay and asked me how I felt about the film.

"It isn't subjective evidence, it is objective," I replied, hoping once and for all to shake his doubts arising from the dual confession. "No person can claim it was doctored, coming directly from ABC-TV, and now I'll be able to use Jim Burnes as a witness. Hopefully he'll testify that Mitchell's statements in the film were voluntary and not coerced. This film may not guarantee a guilty verdict, but it sure will give a jury something to think about. In the end, it could be the most important piece of evidence we have against Mitchell."

The wind soon came out of my sails. As soon as I left O'Connor's office, Patten, who was waiting in the hallway, took me aside.

"Bad news," he said. "Morris Mirsky, George Borges's attorney, called me to say Borges is going to testify favorably for the defense, claiming he never did drive Mitchell to the Kralik house." Patten suggested that I talk to Mirsky about submitting Borges to a lie detector test.

Such was the roller coaster ride of a prosecutor—one minute up, the next plunging down. It was a potentially devastating development, and to nip it in the bud, I took Patten's advice and phoned Mirsky, who agreed to come to my office that evening.

Shortly after I returned to my office, Arnold Bornstein, a reporter for the *Long Island Press*, knocked on my door to show me an ad placed in his paper by Herbert Lyon, Mitchell's attorney. The ad was a search for a person alleged to have picked Mitchell up and driven him home from Flushing to Astoria around midnight on July 19, 1963, the night of Barbara's murder.

"Do you have any comment on the ad?" Bornstein asked me.

"Yes," I replied dryly, "I'll try the case in the courtroom, and not in the newspapers."

There were two possible reasons for Lyon placing the ad, I figured. First, it could be the start of a campaign to influence newspaper articles and slant them toward Mitchell on the eve of the trial, thereby affecting the prospective jury's thinking. I quickly ruled this out, since the press was already slanted in Mitchell's favor; indeed, one reporter, Edie Cahill of the *World Telegram*, was believed to be doing some investigation for the Mitchell defense. The second, more likely reason was that Lyon already had such a witness and would produce the ad during the trial to show how the witness was discovered.

The trial, scheduled to start in a few days, was a pot of boiling water about to spill over, and I had no idea if I would be scalded. What other surprises were there in the works?

It didn't take long to find out. While I was pondering how to cross-examine Lyon's mystery witness, I received a phone call from Frank O'Connor asking me to come up to his office right away. When I arrived, Frank Cacciatore and Ben Jacobson, chief of the Appeals Bureau, were already there.

"Judge Shapiro has suggested I grant immunity from prosecution to Winston Moseley for the killing of Barbara Kralik," the Chief said. "If I do, Moseley will surely testify at the Mitchell trial that he, Moseley, killed Barbara, because he'll have nothing to lose. Shapiro feels it would be inconsistent for the District Attorney to prosecute Mitchell while still holding the door open to prosecute Moseley for the same crime. We're legally obligated to provide the defense with any exculpatory evidence. Shapiro is right; it should be done in the interest of justice. After all, it's a jury's responsibility to find the truth; we shouldn't try and withhold evidence they're legally entitled to hear."

After feeling out Jacobson and Cacciatore for their opinions, O'Connor turned to me. "What would you like to do, Charlie?"

"The damn confession is hanging over our heads like a sword," I shot back. "If we let it in, it will probably result in an acquittal; if we don't let it in, we'll be accused of withholding material evidence. I say grant the immunity—then nobody can say we weren't fair. If we get a conviction, there can be no argument the defendant didn't get a fair trial. I never believed we would be able to keep the jury from learning of Moseley's confession anyway. But before you decide, let's wait until Moseley takes the stand, and see how it goes. We can always grant him immunity at that time."

If there was to be a grant of immunity, O'Connor assured me, he would personally come into court and put it on the record.

I was annoyed. "I bet O'Connor would vote for acquittal if he were on the jury," I muttered to Cacciatore on our way out of the Chief's office.

When I returned to my office, Morris Mirsky was waiting for me. I had met Morris shortly after being sworn in as an assistant District Attorney. He had a deserved reputation in Queens as a lawyer who could be trusted and who wouldn't blindside an adversary.

I asked him if he had any objection to my questioning Borges and submitting him to a lie detector test under Patten's supervision. "No," he answered, and we agreed to meet the next morning at the House of Detention in Brooklyn, where Borges was being held awaiting trial on his burglary indictment.

I met Mirsky early the next morning, and while waiting for a correction officer to bring Borges to a counsel room, I received some disturbing information from the correction captain on duty. Although the Department of Correction had been ordered to keep Mitchell and Borges separated, this hadn't been done, and the two had had ample opportunity to speak with one another. Undoubtedly Mitchell had managed to influence Borges; this had to be the reason for his change of mind, I thought. I called O'Connor, who said he would call the corrections commissioner of the City of New York to ensure that in the future the department would comply with our instructions to keep the two boys apart.

Shortly thereafter, Borges was brought into the counsel room where Mirsky and I were waiting. Borges was a short and pudgy sixteen-year-old. I had heard that despite his tough, streetwise appearance, he usually followed Mitchell's lead.

"Are you going to deny driving Mitchell to the Kralik house?" I asked Borges.

"Yeah," he said.

"Did you speak to Mitchell recently and discuss your testimony with him?" He admitted he had. I asked if his conversations with Mitchell had changed his mind about testifying, but he didn't respond. "Listen carefully," I went on, "all I'm interested in is the truth. Are you willing to take a lie detector test?"

Borges agreed after looking at Mirsky, who nodded affirmatively. Mirsky and I left Borges in the hands of a polygraph expert often used by the FBI and went for coffee. When we returned an hour later, Borges said without being asked, "The truth is I drove Mitchell to the Kralik house in the middle of the night. While I waited in the car outside, I saw him climb in the house through a front porch window and come running out a short time later, jump in the car, and tell me, 'I just stabbed a girl.'"

"Is that the truth?" I asked.

"Yes."

I showed Borges the two statements he had given to Pryor and Palmer saying that he had driven his friend to and from the Kralik house on the night of the murder and asked him to read them.

"Are those statements true?" I asked.

"Yes," he replied.

I gave copies of each statement to Mirsky, who agreed to review them with Borges before he took the witness stand.

Borges's agreement to testify and place Mitchell entering and leaving the Kralik house gave me a little more breathing room. Perhaps it could help neutralize or even lessen the effect of Moseley's confession. The Mitchell film and Borges's testimony certainly justified proceeding with the trial.

Now that I had all my witnesses lined up and prepared, it was time to turn my thoughts to jury selection. Somehow I had to minimize the effect on the jury of Moseley's confession to killing Barbara, to prevent it from becoming the controlling fact in the case. In considering prospective jurors, I needed to drive home two points: that they had an obligation to find an explanation for the vicious killing of a fifteen-year-old girl, and that the trial was a search for the truth. Jurors would have to look at all the evidence, including the film of Mitchell's confession and every word of testimony. If they did, Moseley's confession, while it would undoubtedly influence deliberations, might not be the decisive issue.

Given the time constraints, I was as prepared as I could be, and with only one day remaining before the trial began, I decided to take it off. Bernice took the kids to her parents for the day, and I lounged around, watching a baseball game on television and trying not to think about the trial. Of course, it was impossible. I had a nagging feeling that I'd missed something during the preparation, but I couldn't pinpoint what it was.

CHAPTER NINE

Though the usual court buffs were nowhere to be seen on jury-selection day—they knew Judge Shapiro's practice was to clear the courtroom during this preliminary phase—the hallway outside the courtroom was jammed with rubbernecks. It was as difficult to maneuver through the bodies as it had been during the opening day of the Moseley trial.

When I finally made it into the courtroom, I informed Judge Shapiro's personal aide, Edward Welstead, that I wanted to see the judge with Herbert Lyon, Mitchell's attorney. Shortly thereafter, Lyon and I were ushered into the robing room where Shapiro was poised to enter the courtroom.

"Are both sides ready to proceed?" he asked.

"The People are ready," I replied, "but there's a problem you should consider before starting the trial. The Supreme Court is expected to hand down a decision on confessions almost any day. It may require a new procedure during a trial for determining the voluntary nature of a confession. In view of what the defense will undoubtedly argue, perhaps we should wait until the decision is handed down before starting the trial."

Shapiro's response didn't surprise me. "We're going ahead. If the Supreme Court's decision does affect our trial, I'll handle it. I've already sent for a jury panel to fill the room. We'll start as soon as they arrive."

As expected, Shapiro took over much of the process of jury selection.

Limiting his questions to each prospective juror's pedigree, background information, and family structure, he didn't appear to be leaning in any direction, and I felt a certain sense of relief.

When it was my turn to question prospective jurors, I asked them if they had conscientious objections to the death penalty. My purpose was merely to get a feeling about them from their answers. I had no intention of seeking the death penalty in this case for two reasons. First, I didn't believe Mitchell's actions were premeditated and deliberate—both essential elements in proving murder in the first degree—and second, he was only eighteen years old at the time the crime was committed.

I spent most of my allotted time questioning prospective jurors about what most concerned me: making sure the jury saw the trial as a vehicle to seek out the truth and find an explanation for Barbara's killing. As expected, Judge Shapiro rushed me along, and I had to wind down the questioning before completing my task. There were two women on the panel, and I didn't believe either was strong enough to sway a jury. However, I was confident that at the very least one juror would be strong enough to hold out for conviction and perhaps even swing the jury in his direction.

Now it was Lyon's turn to question prospective jurors. A stocky man in his late forties with pronounced jowls, he was one of the slowest-moving people I had ever seen. As he made his way around the defense table and moved toward the jury box, it looked as if his every step was a painful ordeal. Considered one of Queens's premier defense attorneys, he had never been an adversary in any of my prior trials. Of course, I had spoken to the other trial assistants in the office and had been thoroughly briefed on his technique. He was slow and cautious in his presentation, deliberate and very articulate. When he made an objection, it was general in nature, and he always tried to slip in a little speech for the benefit of the jury. I hoped that Shapiro's penchant for expeditious trials would rein Lyon in, but I suspected that in this case, Lyon would be given some latitude. After all, Shapiro believed an acquittal was probable, perhaps even justified.

Shortly after Lyon began questioning prospective jurors, my suspicion was confirmed. The defense counsel was being given much more time than I'd been permitted. Lyon didn't question the jurors as I had done; he made speeches, almost as if he were delivering a summation to the jury. I considered objecting but decided to restrain myself for the time being. Just when I thought Lyon was finishing his first round of questions, he threw out the name of Annie Mae Johnson.

Unable to hold back any longer, I jumped to my feet and interrupted, "Objection." I had always intended to prevent her name and the erroneous autopsy from being raised in the Mitchell trial, and I had to know at the outset how Judge Shapiro would handle this matter.

As soon as my objection was made, the judge called a recess and summoned Lyon and me to his robing room.

"What's the basis of your objection?" Shapiro asked me.

"There's no legal connection between the Johnson homicide and the Mitchell case," I argued. "Defense counsel is trying to use Moseley's true confession about how he killed Annie Mae Johnson to support his questionable statement about killing Barbara. Further, it is double hearsay evidence, an out-of-court statement offered to establish the truth of another out-of-court statement."

Shapiro mulled this over for a few minutes, an uncharacteristic delay. At last he spoke: "There can be no reference to Annie Mae Johnson, her death, or the autopsy during jury selection or in the trial without the defense making an offer of proof outside the presence of the jury."

This wasn't the ruling I was hoping for. I wanted to keep the Johnson autopsies out altogether. So I said to Judge Shapiro, "This is an issue you can decide now. There is no secret what the evidence consists of—statements made by Moseley to the police and Assistant DA Chetta about how he had shot Annie Mae Johnson with his 22-caliber rifle and the autopsy reports, the botched one and the correct one."

Shapiro turned to Lyon. "Will any offer of proof you make on trial contain anything related to Annie Mae Johnson other than what Skoller just mentioned?"

"That's all there is," Lyon admitted.

And so Shapiro decided no evidence would be permitted during the trial about the death of Annie Mae Johnson or her autopsy reports. It was an important ruling, one that enabled me to devote my time to other legal issues sure to be raised during the trial. It also gave me some hope that Shapiro would be neutral in his approach, despite his skeptical attitude about police testimony.

When we returned to the courtroom, my hope died. Lyon was permitted to continue his questioning of potential jurors unfettered by the limitations Shapiro had imposed on me. Lyon concentrated on Winston Moseley and his statement that he had killed Barbara Kralik. I made no objection and tried not to display any emotion in the presence of the jury panel.

When Lyon finished his initial voir dire, I challenged several jurors, as did Lyon, and their replacements were selected. I began the next round of questioning by asking each juror if he or she would accept as factual any statements made by a convicted murderer before determining their truthfulness and any motives that might explain why the statements were made. Again, I was emphasizing the jury's obligation to search for the truth.

At the conclusion of jury selection, which lasted only one day, the jury consisted of ten men, two women, and two alternates. Instead of recessing for the day, Judge Shapiro directed us to make our opening statements. I didn't make a detailed statement but merely outlined what I expected to prove. I didn't mention Winston Moseley at all, not being sure how he would testify on the witness stand. He could admit killing Barbara or perhaps deny it. At the end of my opening, I emphasized the fact that what I had said, and what Lyon would say, wasn't evidence or proof of anything. The jurors, I reminded them, had to keep an open mind and not form any opinions until the start of deliberations; they had to bear in mind the importance of searching for the truth. Much to my surprise, Shapiro didn't cut me off.

Lyon's opening statement was sketchier than I'd expected. He passed over the subject of Moseley almost casually, and I realized that he, too, was being cautious, not sure of how Moseley would testify. If Moseley didn't admit to the killing, it would seriously weaken the defense.

Instead, Lyon concentrated on the police investigations and the claim that Mitchell's confession was involuntary and the product of physical abuse, long periods of intense questioning, and brainwashing. As I listened to Lyon's efforts to take apart the police investigation, I thought about Captain Timothy Dowd. Hopefully his calm and gentle demeanor would make it difficult for any jury to consider his testimony to be anything other than the truth.

After court recessed for the day, I went to see O'Connor, who expected to be briefed at the end of each day. It was a burden on me, considering the time limitations I was already laboring under, and I asked him if I could brief him by telephone from home late in the evening rather than in his office. Fortunately, the Chief agreed.

When I returned to my office, Joseph and Marie Kralik, my first witnesses the following morning, were there. Their testimony had required little preparation, since the night and early morning hours of July 19 and 20 were indelibly etched into their memories. There were no discrepancies in their details of the events of that night. Still, I had two concerns. The first was with Joseph's anger. I didn't want it masked, but neither did I want it to explode in the courtroom. A jury can understand anger by a parent in a homicide trial, but explosive anger can be interpreted as slanting the testimony. Anticipating my thoughts, Joseph told me not to worry; he would keep his anger in check. As for Marie, she suffered from a heart problem and was much weaker than when I had first met her. She was pale, and her eyes were red from crying. I considered not calling her as a witness, but I needed any sympathy her obvious pain could arouse in the jury. Jurors couldn't help but see Marie's suffering as resulting from the loss of her daughter.

As I approached Judge Shapiro's courtroom for the first day of testimony, elbowing my way through the crowd, I noticed that the media was out in full force, representatives from every New York City newspaper as well as some national magazines and television networks. Moseley's trial had been my baptism by fire; this time around, I was more comfortable with the clamor and shoving.

The first day of testimony was uneventful, proceeding as anticipated without extensive cross-examination by Lyon. By the end of the day, four witnesses had completed their testimony: Joseph and Marie Kralik; the medical examiner, Dr. Richard Grimes; and the doctor who was with Barbara at the time of her death. I didn't question Dr. Grimes about any possible weapon other than the scissors. In the event Moseley admitted the killing and described a weapon that Grimes could exclude, I would recall Dr. Grimes later, after the defense closed its case.

That same day the Supreme Court made its ruling on involuntary confessions. A messenger delivered the decision to my home in the early evening. It significantly changed trial procedure dealing with confessions. Until this point in time, it was solely up to the jury to decide whether a confession was voluntary. Now, the trial judge first had to determine whether a confession was voluntary beyond a reasonable doubt as a matter of law before it was admitted into evidence. However, the jury would still remain the final arbiter of the facts in determining whether all or some of the confession was voluntary. In order to comply with the decision, Judge Shapiro would have to hold a hearing out of the presence of the jury. This would delay the prosecution's testimony in the trial proper.

The following morning, I joined Shapiro and Lyon in the judge's chambers. Shapiro, who had a copy of the Supreme Court decision in his hands, informed us he was going to send the jury home for the day and hold a hearing out of their presence. He required me during the hearing to offer into evidence any admissions or statements made by the defendant that I intended to present during the trial.

Shapiro gave me the entire morning to prepare for the hearing. I suspected his largesse had to do with the fact that he himself needed ample time to prepare for such a novel event. After all, as far as we knew, this would be the first hearing of its kind in a homicide trial in the State of New York.

As soon as I was back in my office, I began lining up my police witnesses. I also called Jim Burnes, the ABC reporter responsible for Mitchell's filmed interview, and asked if he could come to my office within the hour. Burnes's testimony was critical, not least because as a reporter who had interviewed hundreds, if not thousands, perhaps he could bolster my contention that Mitchell's statements were in fact voluntary. Burnes arrived less than an hour later. He wasn't hesitant about what he had seen and heard; Mitchell's statements, he firmly believed, had been voluntary and truthful. Why? First, because Mitchell had offered his confession freely, not in response to pointed questions from reporters, and second, because Mitchell didn't have a mark on him, which suggested that he hadn't been abused by the police. Moreover, the defendant looked as if a great weight had been lifted from his shoulder. The latter point, of course, wasn't something Shapiro would permit me to use in court.

The hearing would be a dress rehearsal for the police officers I would later call during the trial. However, any benefit this provided could be overcome by the opportunity it gave Lyon to have two cracks at cross-examining them. If during the trial, any witness gave testimony inconsistent with his testimony during the hearing, the inconsistency could be used to destroy the witness's credibility. And that could have a disastrous effect on the prosecution's case.

As I entered the courtroom for the hearing, there wasn't a vacant seat, the spectators having been permitted to enter before we arrived. Now that jury selection was over, the regular court buffs had resurfaced, taking their place alongside other spectators. I was familiar with many of the buffs from earlier trials. At times, they had useful things to offer, for example, areas of testimony to pursue, predictions on the outcome of a trial, or the length of time it would take a jury to reach a verdict. I made it a point to speak to them at every opportunity.

Today one of the buffs, a retired attorney who had never practiced criminal law, intercepted me as I was heading toward the prosecution table. On several occasions this same man had pinpointed testimony that proved invaluable during my summations.

"We have two pools going," he said. "One is how long the trial will last before Shapiro, and the second is how long the jury will deliberate before reaching a verdict." He paused and then added ominously, "You're going to have a brutal time of it. No one thinks you have a chance."

What he said was discouraging, and I was annoyed that he felt so free to tamper with my hopes before the trial even started. "You've watched enough trials here to know some aren't predictable," I countered. "If this wasn't a homicide case, perhaps I might agree. But it involves the brutal killing of a teenage girl. A jury would have to be insensitive not to try and find the truth."

With that, I made my way to the prosecution table, no more than five feet from the jury box and directly in front of the elevated witness chair some twenty feet away. As I sat down to collect my thoughts, Lyon arrived with his two associates and began his painstaking advance up the aisle, moving slower than molasses in January.

Shortly, Judge Shapiro appeared and rapped his gavel to commence the hearing.

I called Captain Dowd as my first witness.

"Why did you question Mitchell on six different occasions over a six-week period?" I asked him.

"Because, each time we questioned him, he gave us a different version of how he got home on the night of July 19, and we had to check out each version. This took time," Dowd answered.

On direct examination, he presented each and every interrogation of Mitchell flawlessly, without hesitation and in great detail, delivering his account in almost narrative form without too many leading questions from me. In all my trials as a prosecutor, I always tried to let my witnesses tell what happened in their own words, without any interruption by me. In the end, this approach always proved to be more effective; witnesses appeared to be testifying strictly from memory and not according to a preplanned scenario.

Lyon's cross-examination, while thorough, wasn't as probing as I expected it to be, and Dowd's testimony concluded without any holes Lyon could use to support a claim that Mitchell's confession was involuntary.

One after another, I called the detectives who had been active in the investigation, including John Palmer and Chief of Detectives Frederick Lussen. Their testimony was as strong as Dowd's, and Lyon's cross-examinations grew increasingly less thorough. Obviously, he didn't hold out much hope for a ruling that Mitchell's statements had been involuntary.

Instead, Lyon's efforts were directed at eliciting testimony that before Barbara died, she had made the statement to police officers quoted in the *Daily News* immediately after Moseley's arrest about her attacker: "I never saw him before in my life." No doubt Lyon intended to pursue this subject during the trial. Did Mitchell's attorney know something I didn't? To my knowledge, the only statement Barbara had made after the attack was, "It was dark, it was dark." Was Lyon trying to do what I feared all along, to get police officers to say that this statement was a description of Barbara's attacker—a dark-skinned person who couldn't be Alvin Mitchell?

I hoped the next witness would take the sting out of any such impression Lyon may have made. It was Jim Burnes, who testified that although Mitchell appeared to be tired when he was interviewed, there were no signs that he had been beaten or abused. After Burnes's testimony, the hearing was recessed for the day, and I returned to my office where Captain Dowd and Inspector Lussen were waiting.

"Do you know of any statement made by Barbara Kralik other than the one to Detective Fullam?" I asked.

No, they assured me, saying they had spoken to every detective who had or could have had any contact with Barbara before she died.

"I'm worried that information is being withheld from us," I said. "There's the Moseley confession to a police officer who has never been identified and now this. I hope I don't have to face such a dilemma for the first time in the courtroom."

Dowd and Lussen were confident that I wouldn't.

Shortly afterward, Assistant DA Stanley Pryor, the last witness I was going to call during the hearing, showed up to go over his testimony for the following day. We reviewed it carefully, especially the subject of his leaving the room during Mitchell's Q&A. He understood the interruption could be devastating. After all, as chief of the Criminal Court Bureau, he represented the entire prosecutorial staff. I had to put my trust in him. Though he had a reputation for being hardheaded, even the defense attorneys knew they could expect the truth from him in all of their dealings and negotiations.

The following morning, Pryor's testimony went without a hitch, despite some attempts by Lyon to punch holes in his explanation for the Q&A break. The witness vehemently repeated what he'd told me earlier—that the only reason he'd taken a break was to go to the men's room and to allow his stenographer to replenish the paper supply in his stenotype machine. Pryor made it clear that he had no ulterior motive in taking a break. If he'd had such a motive, why would he have disclosed the break in the first place? He could have kept quiet about it, and it might never have come to light. "No person, not myself or any police officer in my presence, struck, threatened, or in anyway suggested any answers to Mitchell," Pryor emphasized, turning to look Judge Shapiro directly in the eye.

With that I rested my case, and Lyon commenced his.

Lyon presented only three witnesses of note—George Borges and the defendant's parents—and none added any fact that might suggest Mitchell's confession was involuntary. During his testimony, Borges claimed, "I was slapped once or twice by a police officer, but I didn't think nothing of it." At first blush, his being slapped could be considered damaging, but it became almost meaningless when Borges admitted that he couldn't identify the man and that "it didn't bother me at all."

Mitchell's parents testified that they had complained to Dowd that their son had a black eye after being questioned. Dowd had denied this when he was on the stand. Mitchell's father, William Mitchell, said he had also complained to a politician in the area but that he hadn't brought his son along, and there was no verification of such a claim.

In the end, no evidence or testimony surfaced supporting defense claims that statements by Mitchell were involuntary, and Judge Shapiro ruled that they were voluntary. All statements, along with the Q&A to Pryor and the filmed confession could be received in evidence during the jury trial, he ruled. Of course, the jury would be the final arbiter of whether these statements or confessions were voluntary or made under duress.

Before recessing court for the day, Shapiro asked Lyon and me to join him in the robing room.

"I want you to understand I expect to complete this trial before the end of June," he said, looking directly at me.

"But Judge Shapiro, that's less than a week away," I objected.

He wasn't interested in further discussion. Clearly, I would be walking a tightrope; my questions on direct examination would have to be limited, because I needed to leave enough time to enter into evidence Mitchell's filmed confession. Without that film, Mitchell could well be acquitted, especially if Moseley took the stand and testified to killing Barbara Kralik.

Later on, in my daily briefing with O'Connor, I aired my grievances about Shapiro's apparent bias. "I'd lay odds that when he charges the jury, it will be comparable to a defense summation. If I were Lyon, I would have waived a jury trial and tried this case before Shapiro without a jury."

Again, the Chief tried to reassure me. "Look, Charlie, everyone believes that Moseley's confession made a conviction in the Mitchell case insurmountable. If Shapiro lets this case go to jury, it will be a major victory. Don't try to figure him out. You'll never know Shapiro's thinking until he acts. He plays his cards close to the vest. Whatever he does, though, you can be sure it's out of sincere conviction. I refuse to believe he would deliberately try to hurt you or the office."

CHAPTER TEN

The trial resumed the following morning. Jammed as always, the courtroom had certain electricity that was absent during the hearing, which was dull compared to testimony before a jury.

Slowly, the jurors filed in to take their seats. As I studied them, they appeared to be a little puzzled or perhaps bewildered. After all, they had not been informed of the reason for the delay in the trial, nor would they be informed of Judge Shapiro's ruling.

My first witness was George Borges. He swaggered up to the witness chair, glancing around the room. I had seen this defiant swagger many times before from young defendants when I'd been assigned to the adolescent court. Certainly, Borges wasn't afraid.

Once he'd testified to his and Mitchell's activities in the early evening of July 19, I asked Borges what the defendant had done after leaving the school.

Without hesitation, Borges answered, "He said he wanted to see this girl sleeping over her friend's house, so I drove him to Springfield Gardens, saw him slide into the front window. He came out running later, jumped in the car, and told me, 'I just stabbed a girl.'"

While I was convinced Borges was telling the truth, I couldn't tell if the jury would believe him. After all, he was awaiting sentencing on his burglary conviction, and although he denied any promises had been made to him—I certainly hadn't made any—the jury had to suspect that he was hoping, by testifying here, to get a break on his sentence.

Lyon was brutal in his cross-examination. But he didn't shake this important witness, who stuck to what he'd said during direct examination, although I had to wince when Borges testified that he'd been struck by a chair at one point during his questioning by the police.

Next up was Detective John Palmer. During his cross-examination, Lyon began trying to prove that Barbara Kralik had provided the police with a description of her killer that differed substantially from Mitchell's appearance. Obviously hoping it would get by me, Lyon slipped in a question.

"Did Barbara Kralik tell you her killer was black?"

"Objection!" I instantly called out, jumping up.

Judge Shapiro immediately called a short recess. As the jury filed out of the courtroom, Lyon and I approached the bench.

"Your Honor," I said, "there's only one statement made by Barbara that I'm aware of, and it wasn't a description; it was merely the statement, 'it was dark, it was dark.'"

"I have information that Barbara said her killer was black," Lyon piped up. "I'm entitled to probe in this area, Your Honor." Lyon wanted me to produce certain police officers to confirm the information he had.

"This is a fishing expedition with no basis in fact," I argued. "Moreover, for it to be admissible it has to comply with the legal requirements of a dying declaration. It falls way short of that. Even if she had made such a statement, Barbara hadn't been informed she was in extremis when she made that statement."

Judge Shapiro decided to hold a brief hearing without the jury present. At the end of the hearing, which lasted no more than an hour, he ruled that any statement made by Barbara was inadmissible, because it wasn't a dying declaration.

He turned to Lyon. "You're not to question any police officer concerning any statements alleged to have been made by Barbara. I'll hold you in contempt if you attempt to do so."

All of the police officers I called as witnesses testified without any serious inconsistencies. No discrepancies arose between what they said before the jury and what they'd said during the hearing. Again, Timothy Dowd was especially impressive. Calm and unruffled, he presented his testimony in a straightforward, soft-spoken manner that I felt would convince the jury of his truthfulness.

"My investigation was slow and methodical in order for it to be as thorough and complete as my testimony today," he said, looking straight at the jurors.

The pretrial hearing and preparation had turned out to be dress rehearsals for the jury trial, providing each officer with the confidence to overcome Lyon's probing cross-examination, making them more effective witnesses.

When it became clear that the prosecution case would be completed quickly, Judge Shapiro asked Lyon how many witnesses he had and how long his defense case would take.

Lyon estimated his case would take a few days. Among others, he intended to call the defendant and his parents and a person he claimed had driven Mitchell home from Flushing on the night of the murder.

"For my first witness," Lyon said, rather confidently, "I intend to call Winston Moseley."

I was not at all surprised. It was a wise move to call him at this time. If he admits to the killing, his admission could take over the entire case; if he denies it, Lyon would have the opportunity to prove earlier statements that Moseley had made to police and others about killing Barbara.

"I've never spoken to or interviewed him," Lyon went on, "and I don't have the slightest idea what he'll testify to. I dare say neither do his attorneys. How long it will take is also unknown. It's my understanding that the District Attorney is going to grant Moseley immunity from prosecution for the killing of Barbara Kralik. Under these circumstances, he can't incriminate himself, and he should be free to testify, but who knows how he'll act, being under a sentence of death."

True to form, Shapiro lost no time. He sent for a Department of

Corrections officer and instructed him to bring Moseley to the court-room from the House of Detention in the adjoining building.

While we were waiting for Moseley, Lyon asked to approach the bench. Shapiro called a brief recess and invited us to his robing room.

Lyon asked that I be ordered to produce a tape recording of an inter-view in which, he claimed, Moseley had detailed the murder of Barbara Kralik to one of his attorneys, Sidney Sparrow.

"I haven't the slightest knowledge of such a recording," I said, caught off guard.

"Well," said Lyon, "the tape's been played for Frank O'Connor and Bernard Patten."

How on earth could such information have been withheld from me?

"Your Honor," I said, trying to keep calm, "may I have a few minutes to find out if this tape exists?"

Right away, while still in Shapiro's robing room, I put in a call to Frank Cacciatore.

"The tape does exist," Frank said, "but I've never heard it. I believe O'Connor and Patten have."

Shapiro gave me an hour to find out all I could about the tape. Ten short minutes later, I practically burst into O'Connor's office, trying to control my anger. Bernard Patten and Cacciatore were there with the Chief.

"Sometime in late April," O'Connor explained almost apologetically, "I received a phone call from Sidney Sparrow. He told me he had tape-recorded an interview of Moseley in which he detailed killing Barbara Kralik. Sparrow suggested that I listen to the tape with Patten. However, there were several conditions. The tape couldn't be seen or heard by any other members of the staff or even disclosed, except to Cacciatore. It couldn't be deemed a waiver of the attorney-client privilege or the privi-lege against self-incrimination, and Sparrow would retain possession of the tape. In view of our finding Moseley's confession to killing Annie Mae Johnson to be true, we believed the tape could help us determine if Moseley's statement concerning Barbara Kralik was also true.

"I had to agree to Sparrow's conditions in the interest of justice. Patten had to hear the tape so he could continue his investigation into the Kralik killing. It was this tape and your recommendations that helped me decide to proceed with the Mitchell prosecution. As far as I know, Sparrow still has the tape, and you can report this to the court. Be careful to inform Shapiro that only Patten and I have heard the tape. I don't want the promise I made to Sparrow not to disclose to be compromised."

What could I say to counter this? Sparrow had tied his hands.

"Sparrow must have disclosed the existence of the tape to Lyon," I said. "At the very least, there should have been an understanding that in the event the tape was disclosed to Mitchell's trial counsel, you would be free to disclose it to me. What if Moseley refuses to testify during the trial? Lyon will demand that the tape be played for the jury. This could be more helpful to the defense than if Moseley took the witness stand and admitted killing Barbara. At least if he testifies, he'll be subject to cross-examination. There's no cross of Moseley on the tape. After all, Sparrow was the only person who interviewed him, and I bet he didn't challenge Moseley."

"Handle it the best you can," the Chief said, "but don't do anything that breaches my agreement with Sparrow. Any disclosure about the tape must come from Moseley or his defense team."

"Well, we better get moving," I said. "Moseley's being brought over from the House of Detention as we speak. You'll have to ask Judge Shapiro to grant Moseley immunity from prosecution in the Kralik murder."

By the time we reached the courtroom, Moseley was there, under heavy guard, along with his three attorneys, Sparrow, Sidney Liss, and Martha Zelman. The courtroom was packed, the doors were locked, and hundreds of spectators were milling about outside.

Before the jury was brought in, however, Moseley exercised his privilege against self-incrimination by refusing to answer any questions, and so Judge Shapiro recessed until the following morning.

When the trial resumed the next morning, Frank O'Connor requested that Judge Shapiro give Moseley immunity from prosecution for the Kralik homicide.

"The District Attorney is to be commended for making such representation on the record," Shapiro declared. "It would be inconsistent to prosecute another person for the crime and still hold the door open to prosecute Moseley. By doing this, Mr. O'Connor, you free Moseley to testify before the jury so that such evidence is not withheld from them in their search for the truth."

As soon as immunity was granted, the jury was sent for and Lyon commenced his direct examination of Winston Moseley. He was the same stoic, emotionless person he'd been in his own trial, looking none the worse for his sentence of death.

With everyone in the courtroom straining to absorb every word, without emotion or hesitation, Moseley testified that he had killed Barbara Kralik, Kitty Genovese, and Annie Mae Johnson.

I wasn't surprised; no doubt Moseley was still committed to a defense of insanity in the event his conviction was reversed and a new trial ordered. Sparrow had undoubtedly told Moseley the death penalty hearing could be reversed on appeal, because Shapiro prevented him from offering evidence of medical insanity.

Despite Shapiro's ruling at the start of the trial, in another attempt to bolster Moseley's admission to killing Barbara by establishing the autopsy foul-up in the death of Annie Mae Johnson, Lyon asked Moseley, "When you confessed to shooting Annie Mae Johnson, did you know her autopsy reported she had been stabbed to death with an ice pick?"

Without any hesitation or delay, I jumped up, shouting, "Objection!" If the jurors learned, from the autopsy foul-up, that Moseley alone knew how Annie Mae Johnson had died, no doubt they would be convinced that he had also killed Barbara Kralik. Then it would be impossible to avoid an acquittal.

"Sustained," Shapiro ruled and directed Lyon not to pursue that line of questioning.

Though relieved, I was still concerned it would be devilishly difficult to overcome the effect Moseley's testimony about killing Barbara would have on the jury.

Approaching the witness stand, Cacciatore, who we had agreed would handle the cross-examination of Moseley, was determined to ferret out every possible inconsistency between Moseley's statements and objective information we had about the crime. One soon arose.

"The knife you used to stab Kralik, what kind was it and where did you get it?" Cacciatore asked.

"It was a serrated steak knife I took from my house," Moseley answered.

Thank God, I thought. Dr. Grimes had assured me that a serrated steak knife couldn't have caused Barbara's wounds, which, being ovoid and without serrations, weren't consistent with that type of weapon.

In fact, Moseley's statements produced a whole crop of inconsistencies. For example, he said the Kralik home stood in the middle of the block. It was a corner house. He described the weather on the night of the crime as clear and dry. It was rainy. He claimed that, besides Barbara, there had been three other people in the house. There were actually four others. He testified there were only two bedrooms upstairs, but there were three. During the cross, moreover, he didn't testify to the presence of a boy on the porch, as he had during his trial.

By the time Cacciatore finished with him, I was more convinced than ever that Moseley hadn't killed Barbara. My conviction, however, didn't make it any easier to avoid an acquittal for the real killer, Mitchell. Though Moseley's testimony provided me with plenty of fodder for my summation to the jury, it didn't remove the existence of dual confessions. If the jury believed they created reasonable doubt, a verdict of not guilty was inevitable.

While Moseley was still walking toward the door leading to the holding pens outside, Shapiro ordered Lyon to call his next witness. "William Finn," Lyon called out. A court officer opened the door and repeated the name, whereupon a man in his early thirties entered, approached the witness stand, and took a seat. He was a rough but good-looking man with an athletic build and dark blonde hair. So this is the liar Lyon produced as an alibi, I thought, certain that Finn's testimony had been bought and paid for long before the attorney had placed his phony ad in the newspaper trying to locate a person who had driven Mitchell home on the night of the murder.

It came as no surprise to me when Finn claimed to have picked Mitchell up in Flushing sometime around 10:00 p.m. on the night of July 19 and driven him home to Astoria several hours before the murder took place. In terms of time, his testimony seemed consistent with the school burglary committed earlier that night by Mitchell and Borges

Not having had the opportunity to investigate Finn, I couldn't trap him during the cross-examination. All I could do was establish that he was unemployed, had major financial problems, and had no immediate prospects for upward mobility. Finn was neither impressive nor credible. My hope was that the jury would disregard the limited alibi he provided—limited because Mitchell would still have had time to return to Springfield Gardens from his home in Astoria and kill Barbara.

Next up on the stand was Mitchell's father, who supported his claim that his confessions were the product of police threats and physical brutality. He also testified that his son had arrived home before midnight on July 19. William Mitchell was a sympathetic figure and clearly concerned about his son, and it was impossible to gauge his effect on the jurors. As a parent myself, I understood a father doing almost anything to help his son, especially if he believed him innocent. I couldn't help but feel a certain compassion for William Mitchell. However, knowing what I did about Alvin Mitchell's propensity for violence, especially under the influence of liquor, I wondered whether the father ever had any positive influence over his son.

I went out of my way on cross-examining Mr. Mitchell to be probing but gentle and brief. I didn't want to appear to be badgering him, yet I didn't want the jurors to be convinced that Mitchell had arrived home before midnight. I didn't even probe his testimony dealing with the claims his son had been coerced. I had covered this with my police witnesses, who I was convinced were more believable than the father.

Following his father was Alvin Mitchell himself. Approaching the witness chair dressed in a tailored suit, he almost looked the part of a model choirboy, a gentle soul who could do no harm. I trusted that bringing out his violent history during cross-examination would remove this veneer. All eyes were on him as he promised to tell the truth, the whole truth, and nothing but the truth and then took his seat.

After Mitchell gave brief recital of his age, employment, and family history, Lyon asked him the critical question: "Did you kill Barbara Kralik?"

"No, I didn't," Mitchell answered, looking straight at the jurors.

Mitchell had been well prepared. Each time he denied committing the crime, he raised his voice more. As the denials poured out of him, he kept glancing at the jurors, seeking their sympathy. He was making eye contact with each juror, obviously being careful not to drop his eyes or look down at any time.

During his direct examination, Mitchell testified, "A detective told me to say that I had blacked out before the killing. The detective promised I would only be two years in a hospital."

As Mitchell continued his testimony that he signed a confession because the police had worn him down by their protracted questioning and physical abuse, he said, "I had been struck with rolled newspapers and one time had been punched in the eye."

Lyon tried to pinpoint for the jury the time that Mitchell arrived home on the night of July 19 into the morning of the July 20. In doing so, Mitchell committed a major blunder when he testified that he told the police: "I told them it was pretty late, but it wasn't quite light yet. It was about—I told them about 3:30." This statement provided me with the argument that Mitchell had more than sufficient time to commit the homicide and arrive home an hour later, when it would be not quite light yet.

Although my cross-examination was thorough, probing, and deliberately provocative, Mitchell didn't break on the witness stand, continuing to repeat at every opportunity that he "did not kill Barbara" and that he "didn't do it." He also said, "I'd been hit so many times that I forgot by what and who."

I did, however, manage to get him to admit to a history of violence and other criminal acts, many of them committed when he was under the influence of alcohol. Finally, Mitchell admitted, "Yeah, I belonged to a street gang and was in some gang fights." He also admitted to another school burglary in addition to the one committed on July 19.

However, my predicament remained maddening. If only I could get some shred of evidence, in addition to the testimony of George Borges and the police, contradicting Alvin Mitchell's contention that he was home at the time of the crime. If only I could place him near the Kralik house at that time, or establish that he'd arrived home long after the attack on Barbara. Unfortunately, I didn't have the evidence or a disinterested witness who could provide it. Certainly, Lyon would argue in summation that Borges's testimony was influenced by his pending burglary indictment, inferring that he was looking to avoid a jail sentence.

Before Lyon ended the defense presentation, he made a strenuous effort to get into evidence the last words Barbara had uttered about it being dark. Obviously, the statement wasn't a description of her assailant, but Lyon, despite the earlier warning from Shapiro not to raise the matter, kept on referring to it as a description of the killer. He came up against a brick wall; as expected, Judge Shapiro ruled the statement inadmissible. This ended the presentation of the defense case.

It was now time for me to offer in rebuttal testimony and evidence something I had carefully planned for at this point in the trial and what I considered the most important evidence I would introduce. It was, of course, the filmed interview of Alvin Mitchell by the TV news reporter, Jim Burnes. I always considered it to be the foundation of the prosecution case and my only hope of overcoming Moseley's confession. I wanted the film to be the freshest evidence in the minds of the jurors when they commenced deliberations.

After Burnes completed his brief testimony and the film was admitted into evidence, Judge Shapiro ordered the courtroom darkened, and Jack Peters played the film using a sound projector loaned to me by ABC-TV.

I could see each juror lean forward in their seats. The fifty-inch movie screen was some twenty feet away and faced them on a slight angle. But they had an unobstructed view, the sound was loud and clear, and the identity of Mitchell in the film was unmistakable. As it was being played, it clearly showed Burnes asking Mitchell, "Why did you do it?" and Mitchell replying, "She started to scream, I got panicky, [and] I didn't know what I was doing. I remember hitting her but don't remember stabbing her. You know, I just panicked."

Immediately thereafter, without being asked, Mitchell volunteered, "I didn't mean to kill her."

I felt Mitchell's words were indicative of a consciousness of guilt. I could only hope the jurors would come away with the same feeling.

A few other witnesses were trotted out by both sides, but they were insignificant. Both sides had completed all testimony and offering of evidence, and we quickly moved on to closing arguments.

Lyon's summation zeroed in on Moseley's confession in order to instill reasonable doubt in the minds of the jury about Mitchell's guilt. He argued quite effectively, "If Moseley had been apprehended before Alvin Mitchell was arrested and charged, who would I be representing today?" Concentrating next on the police investigation, Lyon attacked the number of times his client was brought in for questioning and the length of each session. The confession, he argued, "was obtained under duress." Referring to Borges, Lyon highlighted his claim that he'd been struck by a chair at one point during questioning by the police. It was a telling point.

My summation outlined the police investigation, emphasizing that it had been handled in a thorough and professional manner. How could the dedicated efforts of 130 detectives questioning over seven hundred people be disregarded? To do so would be to make a liar out of every police officer who had testified and Assistant DA Stanley Pryor as well. I asked the jury to consider the filmed confession of Mitchell.

"It can't lie or be distorted," I said, holding up the can of film. Looking each juror in the eye, I repeated several times, "This may be the most important evidence in the entire case, and it is objective and cannot lie."

"Search for the truth," I urged the jurors. "Find it and then you will convict Alvin Mitchell of the murder of Barbara Kralik."

I sat down, hoping the film would force the jury to try to get at the truth of who killed a fifteen-year-old girl in cold blood.

On June 26, little more than a week after the start of the trial—an extraordinarily short period for a high-profile homicide case—Judge Shapiro charged the jury. His words were as damaging to the prosecution as they could possibly be, openly conveying his mistrust and disdain for police testimony and procedure. Cacciatore, who came and sat next to me during the charge, literally had to hold me down as Shapiro instructed the jury. "This is not Communist Russia or Nazi Germany. The days of the rack and screw are over. If you have any doubts about the manner in which the confessions were obtained, you should throw them out."

My heart sank. I had always believed that Shapiro would leave the door open, allowing the jury to make a good-faith effort to search for the truth. Instead, what he delivered to their door struck me not as a charge so much as a defense summation based on the argument that Mitchell's confession had been involuntary. It was devastating.

Shortly before noon, the jury left the court to commence deliberations. Shaken, I pondered the charge, trying to figure out the judge's objective. The more I thought about it, the more I felt that his sense of justice was genuine. I knew he had doubts resulting from the two disparate confessions. By giving Mitchell the benefit of a favorable charge, Shapiro would have a clear conscience in the event of a conviction.

At 3:30 p.m., the jury reported that they were deadlocked. Judge Shapiro directed them to continue deliberations as they had only been at it for a short time. At 11:30 p.m., they reported they were hopelessly deadlocked, and the foreman declared, "It would be useless to continue arguing."

"I hereby order the jury disbanded and declare this a mistrial," Shapiro announced. He scheduled the case for a retrial on July 6, 1964—the same day Winston Moseley was to be sentenced to death for the murder of Kitty Genovese.

"Congratulations," the Chief said when I called him from a phone booth outside the courtroom to report the results. "You should consider a hung jury a success in light of the Moseley confession. We were right to proceed with a prosecution."

When I emerged from the phone booth, a newspaper reporter approached me and said the jury was deadlocked at eleven to one for acquittal. All I had needed was a single juror, and by golly, I'd gotten one. But it didn't make me feel any better. For the time being, at least, Barbara Kralik's murderer was free, and I didn't know if he would ever be held to account.

The cumulative ordeal of sensational back-to-back trials had left me exhausted, and the next day, O'Connor told me to take a thirty-day vacation. "I'll have the case adjourned until after your return," he said. "Then we'll decide what to do about it."

CHAPTER ELEVEN

I jumped into my car and drove two hours upstate to meet my family in the Catskills, where we'd rented a bungalow for the summer. Over the next few weeks, I studiously avoided reading any newspaper articles about the Mitchell trial. Friends and relatives seemed intent on drawing me into conversation about it, but I refused to respond. After all, it was a pending indictment about which important decisions were yet to be made. I was duty-bound to remain silent. Moreover, I needed an emotional and psychological break from the case even more than I needed sleep.

Try as I might to forget, however, the case kept intruding into my thoughts. I had forgotten that some of the Mitchell files were in my car. Then one day, I took Bernice and the kids shopping. When I opened the trunk to put the packages inside, there were the trial transcripts, nestled inside. I'll just glance over this stuff briefly, I thought, reaching for them, then thought better of it, remembering the promise I'd made to myself to enjoy the family on this vacation. The thought that I could never get out of my mind was how I would feel if it had been one of my children, Beth or Robert or Caren, and not Barbara Kralik who Mitchell had murdered. I would never give up without finding the truth.

By the end of July, I had caught up on my sleep and drove back to Queens, leaving my family upstate for the rest of the summer. The two-hour drive enabled me to concentrate my thoughts on the Mitchell trial for the first time in almost thirty days. I came to two conclusions. First, if there were to be a retrial, I would need much more time for the preparation, most likely several months. And second, I wouldn't rely on the police investigation or Stanley Pryor's Q&A to buttress my case. No, I would start my own investigation from scratch, without police involvement.

I arrived at the office early the next morning for a meeting with the Chief, Frank Cacciatore, and Bernard Patten. I could see that O'Connor wasn't his usual relaxed self.

Leaning forward in his oversized chair, he looked directly at me and said, "Although I'm inclined to dismiss the Mitchell indictment, I haven't made up my mind. I've reviewed the minutes of the Mitchell trial as well as Moseley's testimony at his own trial. I can see the differences between Moseley's confession and the facts surrounding the Kralik killing. I also realize that Shapiro tried the case for a defendant's verdict or, at the least, for a hung jury. But that doesn't eliminate my concern about the possibility of prosecuting the wrong man. I want your honest and open ideas now, because when you leave my office you'll know my decision, one way or another."

Patten and Cacciatore looked at me. "First and foremost," I said, "we owe Barbara Kralik her day in court. That we're facing an apparently impossible task of proving one confession false and one true shouldn't control our obligation to find the truth if we believe Alvin Mitchell killed Barbara Kralik. Second, a new and thorough investigation by our office might uncover some new evidence that the police overlooked. After all, their investigation was based entirely on Mitchell's confession and Borges's statement and ended there. Third, as you point out, Chief, the details in Moseley's testimony about the Kralik homicide differed substantially from the details of that homicide. Fourth, a dismissal by our office doesn't remove the doubts about the police investigation or Pryor's participation in their investigation. Fifth, a new trial judge with an open mind about police testimony wouldn't raise the same questions in jurors' minds that Shapiro's one-sided charge did.

"In short, we shouldn't dismiss the indictment. There must be a retrial and a verdict one way or the other. Without a verdict, you can kiss goodbye any chance we have of finding the truth."

Patten and Cacciatore made the same recommendation, using arguments similar to mine.

"Did you guys meet earlier to gang up on me?" O'Connor snapped.

"No," Patten laughed. "We're just aware of each other's thinking."

Without further ado, O'Connor made his decision. "Go ahead with a fresh investigation, Charlie. However, I'm warning you, unless you come up with something new I'm going to move to dismiss the indictment. Do you have any idea how long it'll take or how much help you'll need?"

"At least several months," I replied. "I'll be looking into three areas. One is finding the person or persons who told Mitchell that Pat was sleeping over that night. The second is trying to put Mitchell near the Kralik house either shortly before or after the crime occurred; I'll go door to door if necessary. The third area involves William Finn, who Mitchell claimed gave him the ride home. Proving Finn lied at the trial will make a liar out of Mitchell and strengthen our case. I need Jack Peters and Harvey Beaber, the county detective who prepared my other cases. I'll use Jack for investigation and Harvey to bring in the witnesses I'll reinterview. I won't involve Dowd or any of the detectives connected to the original investigation. If I come up with anything, I don't want Lyon arguing it's the continuation of a tainted investigation."

O'Connor directed me to start immediately, and I lost no time. By the end of the week, the list of people I wanted brought in to question numbered over a hundred. They included Kralik and Farfone family members, friends and neighbors of both girls, friends of Mitchell and Borges, and neighbors and fellow employees of Mitchell. I would be interviewing them starting on Monday, August 10—twenty people a day, at intervals of half an hour.

Joseph and Marie Kralik and their two sons, John and Lawrence, were waiting for me Monday morning when I arrived in the office. The grandmother was too elderly and infirm to make the trip into the office, and I hadn't included her on my list. The only tidbit of potential significance they provided was the disclosure that prior to the murder, Mitchell had been upstairs more than a few times and in Barbara's room on several occasions, something he had denied under oath at his trial.

The Farfones arrived next, and again, no new facts surfaced that would help my case.

After they left, I began speaking to all of Barbara's friends from Springfield Gardens. This took up the rest of the week, and by the end, I was disappointed and frustrated. While many recalled conversations in the neighborhood about Pat sleeping over at Barbara's house, none could remember if Mitchell had been present at the time, and not one had had a direct conversation with Mitchell in which the subject came up.

Scheduled to appear next were Mitchell's friends. From what I knew, they were a tough, close-knit bunch that had been involved in too many illicit activities to be helpful to any prosecutor or the police. Instead of interviewing them all, I decided to limit my interviews to the two friends who had been with Mitchell in Flushing before he and Borges had burglarized the school and returned to Springfield Gardens. Both young men said they didn't know where Mitchell and Borges went after leaving Flushing.

And so it went. By the end of two weeks, I had interviewed close to seventy-five people and come up empty-handed. I decided to hold off on additional interviews until I had reviewed the entire Mitchell file with a fine-toothed comb, including the trial transcript.

In the interim, the Mitchell case was assigned for trial to Justice Edward Thompson, a former New York City fire commissioner who had recently been assigned to the supreme court. Judge Thompson, still cutting his teeth as a criminal trial justice, wasn't anxious to rush to trial, and the case was adjourned to January 1965.

The adjournment gave me some needed breathing room. As I combed through the Mitchell file, Jack Peters was a great help, offering suggestions learned during his many years as a detective, in areas where my investigative experience were limited. But it was to no avail. Several months went by, and not a single shred of new evidence came to light.

It was now November. The trial, in the event O'Connor decided to proceed with one, was only two months away. Increasingly discouraged, I began working on the file in my basement den late into the night and even during the early morning, weekends included. Early one morning, my inquisitive daughter, Beth, now five, came down to the den.

"Daddy, what do you do here at night?"

My eyes were glazed over from staring at the Mitchell file. I took her into my arms, missing the time I could have spent with her had I not been so immersed in this stalemate of a case. "Just working, honey," I replied wearily.

In the midst of my discouragement, I still had the nagging feeling that something had eluded the police and me as well. I didn't know what it was, but I sensed that it might be staring me in the face.

And so I started rereading Mitchell's trial testimony with fresh eyes. And before long, something *was* staring me in the face: Mitchell had testified at his trial that at one time during the investigation, before telling the police he'd been given a ride home on the night of the murder, he'd told them he went home by way of bus and train. He had admitted on cross-examination that no police officer had suggested this to him.

Heart pounding, I reviewed Mitchell's original statement to Detective John Palmer: "Borges dropped me off at a bus stop on Springfield Boulevard, and I took the bus to Jamaica and the subway home to Astoria." Pryor's Q&A confirmed the same statement from Mitchell.

Borges had said the same thing in his own statements and testimony: Mitchell had jumped in his car after running out of the Kralik house, and then Borges had dropped him off at a bus stop on Springfield Boulevard.

Out of the hundreds of DD5s, I couldn't recall any that had mentioned police or detectives searching for a bus driver, train conductor, change clerk, or passenger who might have seen Mitchell in the early morning hours of July 20, 1963. For the tenth time, I reviewed the DD5s. No, not one.

Though it was after midnight, I called Captain Dowd and asked him if such a search had been made. He said he didn't believe so and admitted, "After Mitchell confessed to me and Pryor, the police investigation ended, and the matter was turned over to the District Attorney's office. I assumed Pryor would take over from then on or at least the DA Investigations Bureau."

It was a long shot to come up with a witness sixteen months after the crime, and even if I did, how credible would the person be? Running out of ideas and time, however, I had nothing to lose. When Jack Peters arrived in my office the next morning, I filled him in. "Go down to the transit authority," I said, "and check out all bus routes along Springfield Boulevard in the vicinity of the Kralik house that either ended at or passed by the subway station in Jamaica. At that time of night, there was probably only one bus operating on a route. Maybe we'll get lucky. Check out the subway as well—conductors, change clerks, and the like."

Later that afternoon, Jack called and said, "There was a bus that ran along Springfield Boulevard and passed within a block of the Kralik house. The bus ended its run at the subway station in Jamaica where Mitchell would have traveled by subway to Astoria. There was only one bus on the route from midnight to 7:00 a.m., and I have the name and address of the driver, who's still employed by the transit authority. I also got the name and address of the subway change clerk on duty at the Jamaica station in the early hours of July 20 and of several subway conductors of trains leaving from the Jamaica station and going close to Astoria."

"Start bringing them into my office tomorrow as soon as you locate them," I said, my adrenaline flowing. "If you need any help, ask my county detective, Harvey Beaber. Don't mention the Mitchell case to these people. All they need to know is that we're investigating a crime. I don't want anyone to say we put words in their mouths if they do have information."

The following morning, December 30, Jack arrived at my office with a bus driver employed by the transit authority. His name was James Lewis, and he was a resident of Hollis, Queens. Lewis was a clean-cut, pleasant-looking black man in his early thirties, who had been a bus driver for five and a half years. He worked the graveyard shift, five nights a week, and each night he drove a different route.

"The route along Springfield Boulevard in Springfield Gardens was the Q5," Lewis told me. "I only drove that last summer [the summer of 1963], from late Friday night into Saturday morning." In what Lewis described as his inbound route, the bus traveled within a block of the Kralik home and then on to the Jamaica subway station. "What's this all about, anyway?" he asked.

"We're investigating a homicide that took place in Springfield Gardens sometime in July 1963," I said guardedly. "I want to know if you remember anything unusual happening when you were driving the Q5 route that month."

Lewis took some time before answering, and it was clear to me that he was giving serious thought to his answer. First, he mentioned an incident involving a woman passenger. That wasn't connected to my investigation, I told him.

Then, after mulling it over some more, he said, "I remember one night a young man, about twenty years old, who seemed to be a little drunk, got on my bus at South Conduit Avenue and Springfield Boulevard at approximately 4:15 a.m."

"Can you describe him?" I said casually, trying to play down my keen interest.

Without any hesitation or prompting, Lewis answered: "He was about five foot eight or nine, thin faced, with sandy-colored hair falling a little over his eyes. He was dressed in a black T-shirt and black jeans and had a bloody handkerchief wrapped around his right hand."

Stunned, I almost turned over my chair. Lewis had given me a perfect description of Alvin Mitchell, down to every detail we had learned about his clothing and the bloody handkerchief on his right hand. Detectives had recovered his black T-shirt and black jeans from his parent's home early in the investigation after Mitchell had told them how he was dressed on July 19.

I couldn't believe my ears. Could we be this lucky? What was the likelihood of finding a witness more than sixteen months after a crime who hadn't been turned up by a police task force of 130 detectives?

But Lewis hadn't pinpointed the date. Without it I wouldn't be able to use him as a witness, because his description wouldn't be directly connected to the night in question. Lewis would also have to be able to identify Mitchell as the young man who boarded his bus.

"I'm interested in a Friday night in July going into the early morning hours of Saturday," I told Lewis.

"That's the only night of the week I drove the Q5," Lewis said.

With nervous trepidation, I posed the question: "Do you remember the date?"

"I can't be certain of the date now," he said.

"Okay then, go home, think about it carefully, try and associate it with some event in your life or your family's. If you can piece it together and remember the date, call me and we'll meet again. But please be careful. I'm investigating two unrelated people who have both admitted to killing a girl. We're only interested in the truth and what you know and can remember with certainty. I can't provide you with any information; it must come entirely from you."

After Lewis left my office, I interviewed the subway change clerk and several conductors, but they weren't able to provide any useful information.

I wondered if I should have shown Lewis the ABC-TV film of Mitchell being questioned by Jim Burnes outside police headquarters. If he were able to identify Mitchell, perhaps the date would follow. That would be foolish, I decided. Imagine how Lyon would come after me had I not given Lewis the opportunity to think the matter over before trying to fix the exact date!

I was tempted to call Frank Cacciatore for advice, but he had recently been sworn in as a judge in the criminal court of the City of New York, and I no longer could consult with him. Instead I phoned Bernard Patten to see what he had to say.

"Let me speak to Lewis; maybe it will help him remember," he suggested.

"I did suggest the month we were interested in," I said, "but he wasn't certain of the date, and I decided not to push him. I don't want to contaminate his testimony. The whole case could backfire on us."

Patten agreed. "If he comes up with the date and it fits, you'll have to get a detailed statement from him. I'll do it for you, since you don't have much time before the trial."

Patten also said he would do a thorough investigation of William Finn, the witness who'd testified at the trial that he'd given a ride to Mitchell on July 19 from Flushing to Astoria.

"I want to know everything about William Finn and his family from the time he was born," I said. "But he can't find out he's being followed. I don't want any claims of intimidation or harassment by the police or our office argued during the trial when he testifies. I suspect Finn is a complete phony whose testimony was bought and paid for; find a connection to Herbert Lyon if at all possible. Finn isn't the Good Samaritan type who would pick Mitchell up late at night and drive him to Astoria, an area, admittedly, he was not familiar with. After all, Finn lived in Ridgewood, and Astoria wasn't on the way home from Flushing, where he claimed to have picked Mitchell up."

Patten told me he would start immediately and convene a special grand jury session if he came up with anything.

It was time to let O'Connor know, and I called his office and asked to see him.

"I may have come up with something important," I announced and filled him in on how I'd dug up Lewis and what he'd told me.

O'Connor, looking both interested and excited, asked, "Is it wise to wait to hear from Lewis? Perhaps you should contact him in a day or two and even push him a little."

"Perhaps, but I don't think so. It may be a risk to wait and leave him alone, but I believe it's more dangerous to do otherwise. Lewis is articulate and quite credible. He'll make an excellent witness if he comes up with the date. He seems to have a powerful memory. He knew each route he drove last year, and he drove different ones each night of the week. If he comes up with the date on his own and contacts me for a meeting, Lyon won't be able to attack Lewis's credibility or me. Of course, if I don't hear from him within a reasonable time before the trial, I'll have to contact him. But for now, I'd like to leave him alone."

The Chief nodded. "If Lewis comes up with the date without any pressure from outside, the trial can go ahead. Whatever the result, I'll be satisfied you did everything humanly possible in your investigation."

I tried not to pin all my hopes on Lewis, but it was hard not to. If he contacted me on his own and with the correct date, instead of trying the Mitchell case to prevent an acquittal, I'd be trying it for a conviction.

I asked Jack Peters to start lining up our witnesses, especially the police. I wanted all of them available from January through April. This trial would take much longer than the first. No doubt Judge Thompson, being even more of a neophyte as a criminal trial judge than I as a prosecutor, would proceed more slowly than the rabbit-footed Shapiro would, and examining all the witnesses who had previously taken the stand would be a tedious ordeal. The trial could well last several months.

Not long after asking Patten to investigate William Finn's background, I met with Patten in his office to learn what he'd found out. Apparently Finn was a scofflaw who owed several thousand dollars in unpaid traffic tickets. More revealing was what Finn's own sister had told Patten.

Patten leaned back in his chair, fingers laced together. "She claimed that Finn had stolen money from her on several occasions and had recently removed several valuable items from her apartment, including a TV set and some jewelry. She was about to file a criminal complaint against him when our detectives approached her." He paused. "I think we should submit a charge of grand larceny to a grand jury."

"Don't do that yet," I said. "It might look as if we're intimidating Finn. Go ahead with the presentation to the grand jury, but delay the indictment until after the trial. It would be best if Finn were taken into custody on the scofflaw charges—that way he'll be available and won't disappear. In the event Lyon fails to call him as a witness, I'll try and force Lyon to call him. Then I'll be in a position to discredit Finn and Mitchell at the same time."

"How so?" Patten asked.

"If Lyon doesn't call Finn as a witness, I'll use his failure to do so in my closing arguments to the jury. Not calling a person who's the equivalent of an alibi witness would be tantamount to admitting he was untruthful. That would tarnish both Finn and Mitchell."

Patten agreed. "I'll present the case against Finn to the grand jury tomorrow and ask it to withhold any finding. Do you want to be there?"

"Absolutely," I answered.

Early the next morning, I appeared in the Queens County grand jury room and listened to Patten question Finn's sister, who was quite persuasive. Several jurors wanted to know what this presentation was all about, and Patten explained the circumstances of the Mitchell case—our belief that Finn had perjured himself by testifying that he'd given Mitchell a ride home when in fact he hadn't even known the defendant before the trial. Later the jurors voted to delay any indictment of Finn until after the Mitchell trial. However, Finn was taken into custody by Nassau County Police and held, because he was unable to post bail.

Arnold Bornstein of the *Long Island Press* came to see me the following day. "I'm doing an article based on an interview with Finn," he told me. "Finn complained he was being harassed and followed by the police and the District Attorney's office."

"That's not true," I said. "We were conducting a criminal investigation, and there has been a grand jury proceeding, but I can't comment on it."

The next morning, Bornstein's article, mentioning Finn's complaints and my response, appeared in both the *Long Island Press* and the *Star-Journal*. I wasn't upset by the publicity; I wanted Lyon to find out about our investigation.

With the trial scheduled to start before Judge Thompson in mid-January 1965, time was running short, and the pressure was mounting.

It was January 3, and still I hadn't heard from Lewis. Several times Frank O'Connor asked me how long I would wait before contacting him. I was sorely tempted to call. Several times a day I reached for the phone, knowing the Chief would dismiss the indictment against Mitchell if Lewis didn't come up with the date. Then I would stop myself. Lewis's testimony had to be untainted.

I arrived in my office early on Monday, January 4, after spending the New Year weekend trying without success to fend off thoughts of the Mitchell case. The telephone rang outside my office in the small reception area just as Jack Peters started to brief me on the witnesses waiting in the District Attorney's detective squad room.

"James Lewis is on the line," Jack Peters announced.

My heart was racing as I picked up the phone. "Good morning, Mr. Lewis," I said.

"I remember the date," he blurted out without exchanging pleasantries. "It was July 20, 1963, and there is no mistake about it."

"Can you come into the office right away?" I said, trying to keep calm.

"I'll leave right now."

"Would you like me to send a car?"

"No, I can be there in less than an hour."

I felt lightheaded, hanging up the phone. "Jack," I said like someone in a trance, "keep the witnesses waiting in the squad room. Set up the projector next door, and load the film of Mitchell's confession to Burnes."

True to his word, James Lewis appeared forty-five minutes later. He appeared relaxed while my hands were almost shaking with nervous excitement.

"How did you come up with the date?" I asked after he sat down. "I have to hear the whole story, because it's sure to come out at the trial during cross-examination."

"It's simple," he said. "My wife had a baby on Friday morning, July 19, 1963, and I remember bringing the newspapers to her in the hospital on Sunday night, the twenty first. The murder was all over the paper, including the girl's picture. I just never associated it with the young man who got on my bus the morning of the twentieth."

I leaned forward, looking at him intently. "I know you told me on the phone there's no mistake, Mr. Lewis, but you must understand that two men have confessed to killing this young girl. Your testimony will be key evidence in the trial against one of them. That's why there can be no mistake. If there is the slightest doubt in your mind or memory, you have to let me know now."

"I have no doubt," he said calmly. "The young man I described to you got on my bus around 3:30 to 4:00 a.m. on the morning of July 20, 1963."

"Okay," I said. "I've got a film to show you."

We moved to the darkened office next door, and Jack played the film. The sound couldn't be turned off but Jack kept it as low as possible and the questions put to Mitchell and his responses were still audible.

When the film ended, Jack flicked the lights on, and turning to Lewis, I asked, "Did you recognize anyone in the film?"

He gave me a level look. "The young man in the film who said he didn't mean to do it is the person who got on my bus that morning. There's no doubt about it—that's him."

"You've convinced me, but the chief of our Investigations Bureau, Bernard Patten, wants to meet you and take a statement. Will that be okay?"

The elation I'd been trying to resist prematurely flooded over me and so did some questions. Why hadn't the police located Lewis in the beginning, when they were still investigating the death of Barbara Kralik? It was a grave oversight. And why hadn't I found him—because there'd been so little time to prepare for the first Mitchell trial? I chided myself. If Lewis had been a witness in the first trial, it might have changed the result. The only thing that allayed my regrets was the thought that the combined force of Moseley and Finn's testimony probably would have prevented a conviction. The hung jury would merely have been less lopsided.

I asked Lewis to wait in the outer office and called Patten. Mitchell was due in court the following day to be arraigned on the burglary charge, and Patten and I agreed to have Lewis present when Mitchell was brought before the judge in order to firm up the identification. Afterward, Patten would take an unsigned statement from Lewis.

Next, I called Frank O'Connor with the news. "Do you want to meet Mr. Lewis?" I said.

"It's not necessary," he replied, sounding pleased. "Though the odds were against you, it seems you handled Lewis the right way. You can go ahead and try the case now. What kind of a witness do you think he'll be?"

"Chief," I assured him, "Lewis is more than credible—he's completely convincing. He also has an exceptional memory. With his testimony, we stand a chance of overcoming Moseley's confession."

After hanging up, I called Lewis back into my office and asked him to return the following day at 9:00 a.m. sharp. He showed up promptly. We chatted for about half an hour, during which I carefully avoided discussing his forthcoming testimony, then made our way to a private corridor behind part I of the criminal term of the Queens Supreme Court, where we met up with Bernard Patten. Part I was the largest courtroom in the building, used for arraignments of defendants following indictment.

I showed Lewis to a seat in the front row. From where he was sitting, he would have a clear view of Mitchell's face as he was led in from the holding pen on the opposite side of the room to be arraigned on the burglary charge. There were many arraignments scheduled for that day; Lyon wouldn't know who Lewis was or what he was there for. Concerned that some reporters would make attempts to contact Lewis and perhaps affect his testimony, I didn't want to disclose his identity until the start of the trial, when I would be legally required to do so.

Patten and I withdrew to the private corridor before Mitchell appeared. At about 10:00 a.m., the defendant was brought before the judge. The entire proceeding lasted no more than fifteen minutes, whereupon Lewis met us back in the private corridor.

"Is he the one?" I asked.

"Yes," Lewis said. "That's the person who got on my bus."

With that cleared up, Patten took Lewis to his office for an interview without me. Before leaving, the assistant DA reassured me, to my relief, that he wouldn't ask Lewis to sign the statement. I had purposely not taken any written statement from Lewis out of fear that it could be used by Lyon on cross-examination to attack Lewis's credibility if the statement turned out to be inconsistent with his oral testimony. But at least an unsigned statement would make it more difficult for Lyon to attack him on the witness stand—Lewis could testify he had never seen the statement and never read it.

CHAPTER TWELVE

The Mitchell indictment was adjourned to Judge Thompson's trial calendar for January 18, 1965, and for the first time, I had had more than enough time to prepare.

Among other tasks, I made copies of the testimony of each witness who'd appeared during the first Mitchell trial, turned them over to the witnesses for review, and questioned them in my office once again. Pleased that no conflicts arose between their earlier testimony and their new statements to me, I decided to call as witnesses every person who had testified in the first trial, with the exception of Marie Kralik, who was too ill to appear. After finishing my work with the witnesses, I prepared a new trial brief and added Lewis to the witness list.

One day while reviewing the brief, I received a telephone call from Justice Peter Farrell's legal secretary.

"The judge is on the bench," he said, "but he'd like to talk to you right away."

Surprised, I hurried over to Judge Farrell's courtroom on the third floor of the courthouse.

Peter Farrell was the criminal term's senior judge. Having tried a number of cases before him, I had a healthy respect for his competence as a trial judge, although we disagreed on his sentencing approach. In my opinion, he was too lenient in handling defendants convicted of violent crimes, and he knew how I felt. Farrell and I had had several unpleasant confrontations when he granted probation instead of prison terms to several violent criminals I had prosecuted. As I made my way to his courtroom, I thought he was going to inform me that another judge, not Thompson, would be trying the Mitchell case, perhaps Farrell himself. I couldn't have been more wrong.

The judge was in the midst of a jury trial when I appeared. As soon as he saw me, he ordered a recess and motioned me to follow him to his robing room.

"How's your preparation going for the Mitchell retrial?" he said.

"Fine," I answered.

"Are you ready to go?"

"I think so."

"I understand you have an important new witness in the case. Is it true?"

I reeled back, shocked. His inquiry was highly improper, tantamount to improperly injecting himself into a case for which he had no responsibility.

"Yes," I replied slowly. "How did you find out?"

"Nothing goes on in this building without my knowing about it," he replied smoothly. "What can you tell me about him?"

"Nothing," I retorted, caught off guard. "You're better off not knowing anything about him. In any event, you'll find out soon enough."

His body stiffened, and I could tell he was fuming inside. But I didn't regret my reply. Without question, we both knew it was improper and none of his business.

"The trial is scheduled for Monday, and I still have work to do," I said, then did an about face and left, wondering why he was sticking his nose where it didn't belong.

Back in my office I tried to absorb what had just occurred and what to do about it, if anything. No judge had ever gotten involved in a case of mine that wasn't before him and to which he had no apparent connection. Who would believe me if I reported what had just taken place? It could set off an explosion. There was only one person I could turn to: Frank O'Connor.

I trotted up to his office, and he saw me right away.

"Leave it alone," the Chief said after I explained what had happened. "Chalk it up to curiosity, even though you believe otherwise. Your answer was the proper one. It may alienate Farrell for the time being, but he'll get over it when he realizes he did the wrong thing. Don't worry about it, just try your case. If you have any problems with Farrell in the future, let me know and I'll straighten it out."

I did as O'Connor suggested, though I couldn't resist making a few discreet inquires in the DA's office of a possible relationship between Judge Farrell and Herbert Lyon. All I got back were rumors of a friendship between them, but it was never clearly established.

The next day I awoke with a painful toothache. After taking X-rays, my dentist told me I had an impacted wisdom tooth and referred me to a dental surgeon. What a bad time this had to happen, when I still had some odds and ends to tie up a few days before the start of the trial. That afternoon, under general anesthesia, the wisdom tooth was removed. As if to further frustrate me, the left side of my face blew up to the size of a baseball, and I was in such pain I couldn't even speak. The surgeon advised me to stay home for a week. The tooth had been deeply embedded in my jawbone. He was concerned the jaw would crack, in which case my mouth would have to be wired shut until the break healed.

On Monday, my partner in the office, Edward Herman, made an application to adjourn the case. Judge Thompson granted the application and postponed it eleven days, until January 29.

By Monday the twenty-fifth, I was fully recovered and back in the office to complete my preparation. Late in the afternoon, Judge Thompson's law clerk called to notify me that the judge had signed an order permitting Herbert Lyon to submit Alvin Mitchell to a lie detector test by an examiner of Lyon's choice.

Rattled, I phoned Lyon and threatened to contact the court to rescind the order. Lyon reluctantly agreed to meet me right away in Judge Thompson's chambers.

"Why was an ex parte order signed without my being informed such an application was being made?" I asked Judge Thompson, Lyon by my side.

"I was told you were called, and you didn't appear before me to argue the issue," the judge answered, looking surprised.

"I received no such call! I ask you to rescind the order or at least stay its enforcement until I make application before the appellate division tomorrow morning to set it aside. There is absolutely no purpose to such an order immediately before a retrial. Defense counsel's scheme is to have a polygraph examiner of his choice, with questionable credentials, who will undoubtedly find Mitchell was telling the truth when he said he didn't kill Barbara Kralik. Then Lyon will manage to leak the finding to the press on the eve of jury selection. Your Honor, a long time ago my office offered Lyon the opportunity to submit his client to a polygraph exam performed by the expert used regularly by the FBI, but Lyon refused. I'm confident the appellate division will rescind the order if you don't, Your Honor."

Thompson turned to Lyon. "What do you have to say about this?"

"I don't want to put Your Honor in an embarrassing position. I consent to the order being set aside."

That settled, Lyon and I left the judge's chambers. On our way out, I turned to him. "You keep playing games like this," I said, unable to hide my contempt, "and it will damage your credibility with all the assistant DAs in the office and the judges in Queens as well."

I needed to spend some time thinking about the degree of crime for which I would seek a conviction. It couldn't be murder in the first degree. Mitchell had been drunk and didn't go into the house intending to kill Barbara. He was looking for his girlfriend, and it wasn't until Barbara started to scream that he panicked. Although Mitchell had never said so, I always believed he feared her father would go ballistic if he was found in her room. I'd made a mistake in the first trial trying for a murder one conviction. No, the crime for which Mitchell should be convicted was either murder in the second degree, which didn't involve premeditation and deliberation, or manslaughter, which didn't involve intent to kill. I finally decided not to mention either murder or manslaughter during the trial, especially in my summation. Instead, I would point to the fact that Mitchell had been drinking, asking only that justice be done and the truth emerge, and leave the degree of crime for the jury to decide. In this way, the jury would not be left with the impression that the trial was a personal vendetta, either by the office, the police department, or me.

That Thursday, I received a phone call from Judge Thompson's legal secretary requesting that I attend a conference in his chambers that afternoon with Herbert Lyon. I looked forward to it, hoping to get more of a handle on the judge's style. My only experience with Thompson was the time I'd put pressure on him to rescind his polygraph order. I hoped this wouldn't affect his impartiality in the upcoming trial.

Of course, I had asked a number of people about Judge Thompson, especially assistant DAs who had tried cases before him. Apparently he wasn't either prosecution or defense oriented. He didn't share Judge Shapiro's hostility toward police testimony, nor did he try and take over the lawyers' job of questioning witnesses.

Outside Judge Thompson's chambers, I met Lyon who asked if I would provide him with a list of police officers that he needed as witnesses.

"The Mitchell family doesn't have the money to pay me," he explained, "so now I'm his court-appointed attorney."

I agreed, although I was still annoyed about the polygraph order signed behind my back. Attorneys assigned in a murder case didn't receive sufficient compensation for the responsibility. I knew Lyon would require an investigator at his own expense to determine the names of all the police officers involved in the investigation. I decided that providing the list was the right thing to do and would avoid unnecessary delays during the trial.

After we were seated in his chambers, Judge Thompson graciously offered us tea or coffee. He was a tall, distinguished-looking man with graying dark hair who wore hearing aids embedded in the temples of his horn-rimmed glasses. It was said, on the night before charging a jury, he would attend church and pray for divine wisdom. As New York City's fire commissioner, he'd been an effective administrator. His commissioner's helmet was mounted on a wooden stand on his large desk. Also on display was a large leather-bound book with a cover that read, "Open in case of fire." Anyone who opened the book had these words staring back at him or her in bold print: "Not now stupid, in case of fire."

"I want to lay out a schedule for the trial and get from each of you estimates of how much time will be required to present your side of the case," the judge said.

The trial, Lyon and I agreed, would take a couple of months with four to five weeks of testimony. Judge Thompson gave us a stern look. "I want you in your seats tomorrow at 9:30 a.m. sharp, ready to go. Under no circumstances will there be any continuances. This trial is going to proceed smoothly and without unnecessary interruptions. Of course, this doesn't mean I have any opinion as to whether Mitchell's statements and confessions were voluntary. If I do rule that the People haven't proven them voluntary beyond a reasonable doubt, the case could end on motion of the DA. However, I assume that won't happen. See you in the morning."

Jack Peters and I spent the remainder of the day reviewing my list of witnesses and the list Lyon had handed me. When we left the office at 10:00 p.m., I was confident that the prosecution case was ready and that I had anticipated any efforts Lyon would make to punch holes in the People's case.

CHAPTER THIRTEEN

The following morning at 9:10 a.m., Jack and I stepped into the hallway outside Judge Thompson's courtroom on the third floor of the criminal court building. Before the trial proper, a hearing was to be held to determine whether Mitchell's statements and confessions to the police had been voluntary. Only if the answer was yes would a trial ensue.

This time as I approached the courtroom, my voluminous files and folders were loaded on a gurney. Despite my experience with the sensational Moseley trial, I wasn't prepared for the bedlam we ran up against. The hallway was jam-packed with reporters and spectators vying to get into the courtroom, and once again I found myself fighting my way through the mob, fending off reporters peppering me with questions. I'd promised myself not to discuss the case with anyone from the media until the trial ended with a verdict.

The court officer inside unlocked the door, and as soon as Jack and I rolled our gurney through he clamped it shut again. Presently, Herbert Lyon arrived with his associates, Bill Santoro and Bill Erlbaum. A few minutes later the courtroom was unlocked. In the earlier trial, Judge Shapiro had only allowed ten spectators at a time to be let in; under Judge Thompson there wasn't any such restriction, and the spectators rushed in to grab any available seats. In all, the courtroom could accommodate about two hundred spectators. After the seats were filled, hundreds more were turned away.

Judge Thompson entered the courtroom promptly at 9:30 a.m. Punctuality was one of his personal traits and mandatory for attorneys before him. As soon as he was seated on the bench, he directed the court officers to bring the defendant, Alvin Mitchell, in from a holding cell adjoining the courtroom. The hearing had commenced.

The first two witnesses I called were Detectives William Baker of the 103rd Detective Squad and Thomas Gilroy of the 109th Detective Squad. Their only involvement in the investigation was limited to picking up Mitchell at his home on Sunday, July 21, 1963, and bringing him in to the 103rd Precinct, where they turned him over to other detectives. However, in the car on the way in, Mitchell told the detectives that at around midnight on July 19 he'd arrived in Flushing in the company of Borges.

Surprisingly, Lyon's cross-examination of the two officers was brief and passed over their ride with Mitchell. Both detectives left the witness stand with their credibility intact and Mitchell's statement unchallenged, kindling my hope for an ultimate prosecution success.

My next witness was Detective John Flynn of the Queens Homicide Squad. A police officer for eleven years and a detective for ten of them, Flynn had rapidly advanced up the ranks because of his exceptional conduct. His involvement in the Kralik investigation was minimal. He'd never questioned Mitchell himself, and the only reason I called him to the stand was that his name appeared on the witness list Lyon had given to me, and I wanted to see Lyon's purpose in calling Flynn early on in the hearing.

Lyon's first two questions on cross-examination dealt with other homicide investigations in which Flynn had been involved and which were irrelevant to the Mitchell case. When Lyon attempted to pinpoint one, I objected and Judge Thompson immediately sustained the objection.

Lyon wasted several hours on his cross, often repeating questions, changing only a word or two but not the meaning. It was a method designed to trick witnesses into giving inconsistent testimony, but it didn't seem to be working. Nothing the officer said produced any evidence of use to the defense.

"I can't see what you're driving at," the judge said to Lyon. Neither could I, unless it was another attempt to pursue the statement Lyon claimed Barbara had made before she died.

It appeared as if the defense attorney was grasping at straws. I hoped he continued in the same vein during the trial. Perhaps it would dilute the effect of his cross-examinations.

As the hearing proceeded, the differences between Judge Thompson and Judge Shapiro's courtroom approach became ever more apparent. Whereas Shapiro had pretty much tied my hands on direct examination of witnesses, Thompson was less restrictive and didn't cut off my questioning. Though attorneys aren't permitted to ask leading questions—questions that suggest an answer—of their own witnesses, Thompson gave me room by permitting some leading questions on preliminary or introductory issues. The judge also gave wider latitude to Lyon when he asked repetitious questions. Whereas Shapiro hadn't permitted questioning in areas not directly related to the case, Thompson allowed Lyon to pursue areas far afield.

As Lyon's questioning of Flynn dragged on, it became crystal clear that the voluntariness hearing and the trial, if it took place, would be much longer than I had expected and that the content and approach by counsel would differ from those of the case before Shapiro. My fervent hope was that these differences would land Alvin Mitchell in jail.

Assistant Chief Inspector Frederick Lussen was my next witness, the man who had assigned Captain Dowd to head the task force investigating the Kralik homicide. Lussen's participation in the investigation being minimal—only one day, after which he went on vacation—my questions were limited to whether he or any police officer in his presence struck or threatened Alvin Mitchell or told him how to answer questions. His answers were all negative.

Lyon's cross-examination was what I hoped it would be, its effect diluted as a result of all the time he'd wasted on Detective Flynn. Lyon didn't pursue the question of whether Lussen had placed pressure on Dowd or any of his detectives to conclude the investigation quickly. Instead, the defense counsel confined his questions to why Mitchell hadn't been formally charged with the school burglary after admitting to it on the first day of his questioning.

It was obvious from the bored looks on the spectators' faces—the regular buffs were squirming in their seats—that Lyon was wasting a valuable opportunity to probe for holes in the investigation. With an attorney's dream defense of two unrelated confessions to the same crime, any hole in the prosecution case could open a floodgate and lead to an acquittal.

There were only a few minutes before the lunch recess, and I decided to call Sergeant Thomas Connors of the Queens Homicide Squad. His role was peripheral to the investigation too, and my direct examination lasted less than five minutes. After only a few minutes of cross-examination by Lyon, Judge Thompson called the recess.

No sooner had I stepped out of the courtroom than I was besieged by reporters asking how I felt about the morning session and whether I was confident about the outcome of the trial. I said, "You're going to have to rely on any statements I make in the courtroom during the trial. Just try and be accurate," I responded, directing this last statement to Edye Cahill of the *World Telegram*. Cahill, who had assisted the defense in its investigation, had been writing articles so slanted that they drove one court officer to ask, "Edye, what case are you writing about? It isn't the Mitchell case."

The buildup to the hearing had been exhausting; now that it had started, I was actually relieved. I spent the recess alone in my office, safe from the media, analyzing the morning session and planning my strategy for the rest of the hearing. I decided to limit direct examination of my witnesses and keep my objections to Lyon's questions to a bare minimum. Let Lyon bore the court with his long-winded grasping at straws. This wouldn't help his client one bit. Moreover, the defense attorney's extended cross-examining would have the positive effect of preparing my witnesses to testify before the jury. I had no objection to that.

The afternoon session began with a lengthy cross-examination of Detective Connors, unwarranted by the detective's limited participation in the investigation. Again, no defense points were scored.

John Palmer was my next witness. I spent only a few minutes with him, while Lyon's extensive cross-examination consumed the balance of the first day. Palmer was an effective witness, whose testimony, which went late into the following morning, proved that the time Jack Peters and I had devoted to preparing him was well spent. His testimony describing how Mitchell had pointed out the window through which he entered the Kralik house was helpful. Disclosing the substance of and circumstances surrounding the taking of his handwritten statement from Mitchell buttressed the typewritten statements taken by Assistant DA Pryor. By the end of the first day, I could visualize the direction of the entire hearing. Lyon wasn't going to target the number of hours Mitchell had been interrogated over the course of the five-and-a-half-week investigation as he had in the trial before Shapiro. The defense attorney's original claim of involuntariness was based on the theory that Mitchell was brainwashed as a result of exhaustive questioning. Instead, Lyon would try to establish inconsistencies among the detectives' testimonies. But there was a problem with this approach. All the detectives, except for two, participated at different stages of the investigation, rarely working together.

That evening in my office, I received a telephone message from Joseph Kralik, Barbara's father. Later that night I returned his call. Instead of asking how the hearing was going, as I expected, he gave me some disturbing news. "My wife Marie's heart problems are worse, and the doctor has advised against her testifying at or even attending the trial."

"I'm sorry to hear she isn't well," I said, hiding my keen disappointment. "Marie's testimony isn't critical. I'll try to obtain an agreement from the defense to read her testimony in the first trial to the jury in place of her actual appearance. I'll let you know how it turns out."

Despite my reassurances to Joseph, it was a blow. During the first trial, Marie couldn't have disguised the pain in her face even if she'd wanted to. Her appearance before the jury this time was critical because of the sympathy she would garner, even though Judge Thompson was bound to instruct jurors that sympathy should play no part in their deliberations.

As I approached the courtroom the next morning, there were many fewer spectators milling about outside. I asked one of the court buffs what was going on.

"A lot of people are avoiding the hearing today," he told me. "It's boring, and Lyon is getting nowhere."

The defense continued in the same vein, one witness after another cross-examined with tedious repetition. Lyon did eventually establish the fact that Mitchell had spent many hours being interrogated in police custody, but he didn't seem to support it with testimony proving that Mitchell had been brainwashed or otherwise coerced into confessing.

It took five whole days just to wade through the prosecution witnesses, and this was only the hearing. Then, Lyon commenced the defense part of the hearing. Only two witnesses were called: William Mitchell, the defendant's father, and George Borges. Borges testified that on one occasion he'd been slapped by a police officer, but he couldn't identify whom. As in the first trial, he shrugged the alleged incident off, and it was never connected to Mitchell. With this exception, neither witness offered testimony material to the main issue before Judge Thompson, the voluntariness of Alvin Mitchell's statements.

On February 5, after six days—longer than the entire trial before Judge Shapiro—the hearing ended. Despite Lyon's request that Thompson not do so, the judge read his decision in open court: "The court finds that the People have sustained the required burden of proof, and...that the defendant was neither mentally nor physically coerced into making any statement, admission, or confession...this court...hereby provides the defendant with an opportunity to challenge all of the said statements, admissions, and confessions before the jury itself. Trial before a jury is set for February 8."

One of the first things a trial lawyer learns is that dates aren't set in concrete. Just before jury selection began, Lyon asked Judge Thompson for a one-week trial adjournment, indicating he was contemplating a change of venue. The newspaper articles reporting Thompson's decision that Mitchell's statements had been voluntary were prejudicial, he argued, and created adverse publicity that could unfairly influence a jury. I had no objection to a brief adjournment, and Judge Thompson fixed Wednesday, February 10, for the start of jury selection in the event Lyon didn't move for a change of venue.

As it turned out, Lyon decided against a change of venue. I asked him if he would consent to have me read to the jury Marie Kralik's testimony from the first trial.

"Not without some medical testimony to support the claim that she's too ill to attend the trial," he replied.

And so I got in touch with Marie's personal physician, Dr. David Rothstein, who informed me that his patient had been hospitalized in recent months and couldn't appear in court. He would be willing to appear and so testify.

When I told Frank O'Connor that the trial would start the next day with jury selection, he passed along the finest compliment I was to receive as an assistant DA. "I recently had dinner with Judge Shapiro and Judge Livoti," he said. "Both agreed that because of your thorough preparation of the facts and the way you pursue your cases, of all my trial assistants you're the one most likely to salvage what everyone believes is a losing cause. And you know what? I think they're right. Whatever approach you take during the trial is okay with me. I never expected you to get this far. Frankly, any conviction would be a vindication of the police and would justify our investigation of Moseley's confessions. Continue with what you're doing and I'll never second-guess you on it."

That evening at home, as I briefly looked in on my children at their antics; I hoped they hadn't been affected by my lack of involvement in their lives during the many months of being immersed in the Mitchell case. The only family function I had attended in almost a year was a brief visit to my younger brother Irwin following the birth of his first child, and I longed to spend more time with family.

Putting my regrets aside, I made my way to the basement den for a brief analysis of the upcoming trial. I was standing on much firmer ground in this second Mitchell trial. Surely the bus driver would be the main difference this time around, unless—and this was a matter for speculation—Moseley through some change of heart testified that he hadn't killed Barbara after all. This time around, too, I would be able to argue that William Finn, who Mitchell claimed had given him a ride home, was an outright liar, whose testimony had probably been bought and paid for. Just thinking about cross-examining Finn whetted my appetite.

CHAPTER FOURTEEN

Jury selection would take place in the large courtroom on the first floor of the criminal court building. The room was massive, taking up almost a third of the courtroom space on the first floor. It could accommodate between three and four hundred spectators. When I arrived it was already jam-packed with spectators, who were restricted to one side of the room. The other side was reserved for prospective jurors, who would be sent for as soon as Judge Thompson convened the court. A panel of at least one hundred jurors was needed for the start of jury selection. Many more would be needed before a jury was finally selected.

To my surprise, I felt quite at ease. The jitters that had accompanied me into Judge Shapiro's courtroom were gone, and I had much more confidence. Not only was my case stronger, but now that I'd run the gauntlet of the Genovese trial and survived the first Mitchell trial, the press articles could no longer mention this being my first murder trial as lead prosecutor.

As soon as the first jury panel was seated, the clerk called the court to order, and Judge Thompson took the bench. Unlike Judge Shapiro, Judge Thompson didn't start or take over the questioning; he left the entire voir dire to us attorneys. As the indictment still charged murder in the first degree with a maximum penalty of death, each side was permitted thirty peremptory challenges, which allowed an attorney to excuse a juror without specifying any legal reason.

In my questioning, I concentrated on preparing the jurors for Lewis's testimony. Would the juror consider the testimony of a witness who hadn't testified at the first trial and who was discovered more than seventeen months after the crime was committed? In an effort to discredit Mitchell's so-called alibi witness, William Finn, I asked every potential juror his feelings about witnesses whose testimony was bought and paid for. There was another, more subtle purpose to my questioning in this area, which was to discourage Lyon from calling him as a witness. Finn was being held in custody while awaiting trial on various charges. During the trial, I intended to have Finn kept in a holding cell outside the courtroom. In the event Lyon failed to call him as a witness, I would use this glaring omission as a potent argument during my summation to the jury.

As he did during the jury selection before Judge Shapiro, Lyon concentrated on Moseley's confession to killing Barbara. It was a risk. What if Moseley took the stand and testified that in fact he hadn't killed Barbara? Lyon had no idea how Moseley was going to testify, because Sidney Sparrow, his lead counsel, had denied access to the convicted murderer. Moseley refused to speak to Lyon or to me.

There were several possible defense-leaning jurors I would have liked to excuse but couldn't after running out of peremptory challenges. Fortunately for me, Lyon excused these very jurors. I couldn't help but think he'd wasted his remaining peremptory challenges on them. The final jury, all male, was an interesting blend of law-and-order oriented residents, for the most part coming from areas of Queens with a high percentage of conservative Republican voters, such as Ridgewood, Glendale, and Maspeth. It seemed pretty certain that they would be more receptive to prosecution than to defense arguments.

That night I went home to mull over how to end my opening statement. My aim was to leave the door open for a conviction of either manslaughter or murder in the second degree. What I had to avoid was telling the jury that at the end of the trial they would be convinced beyond a reasonable doubt of Mitchell's guilt. This would have been tantamount to asking for a murder one conviction. Instead, I finally decided,

I would end my opening by walking toward the defense table, pointing at Mitchell and saying, "There sits a killer."

With my case prepared and this final decision made, I spent the rest of the evening thinking about Barbara Kralik's tragic end. How unfortunate it would be if her true killer was acquitted because Moseley, a serial criminal, was using the crime to support an insanity defense.

I had tried the first trial for one juror, to protect the DA's office and the police department. Now, I would pursue the second trial for a conviction of Alvin Mitchell, the person I had no doubt was the killer of Barbara Kralik.

CHAPTER FIFTEEN

Bright and early the next morning, February 18, I arrived at my office for the first day of testimony. Jack Peters, Captain Dowd, and the witnesses I expected to call that day started straggling in shortly thereafter. I was about to leave for the courtroom with Jack and several witnesses when Judge Thompson summoned me to his chambers for a conference with Lyon. I sighed. "What now?" I thought.

When I arrived, Lyon was chatting with the judge.

"Defense counsel wants to make a motion requesting a hearing to obtain information from certain police officers concerning Moseley's confession to killing Barbara Kralik," Judge Thompson told me.

Was Thompson listening to Lyon for the second time without my being present the product of the judge's naiveté, or was it because of his inexperience as a judge in a murder case? I was quite annoyed and decided to let Judge Thompson know it.

"Your Honor, if Lyon has any motion to make, it should be in open court, on the record. Frankly, counsel shouldn't have asked you to sign an order for Mitchell's lie detector test in my absence, and he shouldn't have made this request in my absence either. During a trial there shouldn't be any communication between an attorney and the court without both sides present."

I was between a rock and a hard place, lecturing a judge who was new to the bench, but the law was the law. Expecting Judge Thompson to take offense at this remark, I was surprised when he said, "You're right, Mr. Skoller. Mr. Lyon, make your application on the record. No more conferences here in chambers. See you both at 9:45 in the court-room."

Back in my office, I gathered my files for the day, and Jack Peters piled them onto the gurney. Then we escorted our witnesses for that day to a witness room adjoining the courtroom on the third floor. Judge Thompson had opted to use his regular courtroom as opposed to the large one where jury selection had been held. A poor choice, I thought, as there was sure to be a mob. How right I was. The noise on the third floor was deafening as spectators pushed and shoved to get as close as possible to the locked courtroom doors. A court officer scanned the crowd through a small oval window. The witness room was also packed, and Jack had to chase the spectators out to make room for our witnesses.

Thank goodness for Jack Peters. At no time during the previous Mitchell trial had he left my side, except when I was at home, and there was no reason to doubt that he would be equally reliable during this second trial. Every morning, Jack picked me up in an unmarked police vehicle, and every night he drove me home. The security was comforting.

But there was no security in the court building with the milling crowd. I'll have to bring this to Judge Thompson's attention, I thought. I didn't want to have to fight my way to the courtroom every day, nor did I want my witnesses to feel threatened by the pandemonium before they testified.

The court officer let Jack and me in the courtroom, and we set up the prosecution table. Herbert Lyon arrived shortly thereafter, and within a few minutes, the spectators were scrambling for seats, which filled up in the blink of an eye. Who could blame these people? There is more drama and tension in a murder trial, especially a notorious one, than in any blockbuster movie.

After warning the crowd that no one was permitted to stand or to leave the room during trial proceedings, the clerk convened the court, and Judge Thompson made his appearance.

Dressed conservatively in a sport jacket, slacks, shirt, and tie and appearing surprisingly calm, Mitchell was brought in from the detention pen adjoining the courtroom. Lyon immediately made his motion requesting a hearing. He demanded I produce certain police officers that were present when Moseley first confessed to killing Barbara Kralik. The motion didn't concern me. The hearing wouldn't produce any information that Lyon could use. No doubt the motion was just a tactic to highlight Moseley's confession for the benefit of the multitude of reporters in the courtroom. Lyon wanted headlines about the confession. Playing the media had been a key part of the defense strategy in the trial before Shapiro, and I expected it to be no different during this trial.

Judge Thompson granted the motion, ordering me to produce five police officers for a hearing to be held at some later point in the trial, then directed me to make my opening statement to the jury.

Keeping it brief, to contrast with what I had no doubt would be Lyon's laborious opening, I outlined the crime that I contended had been committed by Alvin Mitchell. It was similar to my opening statement in the trial before Shapiro, with one exception. While scanning the faces of the jurors, I pointed a finger at Mitchell and approached the defense table where he was seated.

"The People will prove," I said slowly and emphatically, my voice raised, "that between 4:15 and 4:20 a.m. on July 20, Alvin Mitchell boarded a bus in Springfield Gardens dressed in a black polo shirt and black pants, with his right hand wrapped in a bloody handkerchief."

At once, a buzz rose from the ranks of the spectators, especially the media. I paused to let it sink in and then moved closer to the defense table. Finger still pointed at the defendant, I looked first at him, then at the jury and declared, "You'll be convinced by the end of this trial beyond a reasonable doubt that there sits a killer, and Lady Justice can continue to hold her head up with pride."

As expected, Lyon's opening statement was much longer than mine. The defense attorney devoted a great deal of time to describing what had taken place in the Kralik house before, during, and after the attack on Barbara.

Stopping for a moment to stare at the jurors, Lyon raised his voice and announced, "This is the morning of July 20. Barbara expired during that day. I think it was at 3:40 in the afternoon. Before she did, she was questioned as to whether or not she could describe her assailant, and she gave some description of an assailant." Surely, I thought, this would be impossible for Lyon to prove, as it was in the first trial. Even if the victim's statement to Detective Fullam, "It was dark, it was dark," had described her assailant, which it didn't, Shapiro had ruled in the first trial that the statement was inadmissible, because it didn't comply with the legal requirements of a dying declaration. In any event, I had to prevent testimony about Barbara's last words from coming out, because Lyon would surely attempt to distort them. Moseley's confession had already sown enough confusion in this case. I couldn't afford any more.

Next, Lyon gave a preview of what Mitchell would claim were his actions on the night of July 19. Oddly, the defense attorney actually admitted that his client had given conflicting stories of how he traveled home in the wee hours of July 20.

Up to this point, I hadn't objected too much to what Lyon said. That changed when he ventured into the circumstances surrounding Annie Mae Johnson's murder and the erroneous autopsy report.

Moseley, Lyon said, claimed he had killed her by shooting her six times, and not by stabbing her. He added, "I intend to show, in relation to the investigation and the care, and the good faith of the investigation of Alvin Mitchell, that the statement as to killing Barbara Kralik was not reduced to writing, but that the other statements were reduced to writing, that the Annie Mae Johnson murder was checked out, and it was found that she was shot, even though the medical examiner had said she was stabbed."

Instantly, I jumped up. "That's objected to again, Your Honor, and I ask it be stricken and I ask Your Honor to instruct the jury to completely disregard it." I didn't know whether Thompson was familiar with Shapiro's ruling in the first trial, and it was a relief when he responded without hesitation, "Strike it out, jury will totally disregard it, nothing to do with this case. Go ahead."

As in the first trial, this was a key ruling. Had it gone against me, such evidence would unquestionably have bolstered Lyon's argument in support of reasonable doubt.

It was no surprise that Lyon ended his opening with an attack on the credibility of George Borges, who would testify that he'd driven Mitchell from the scene of the crime and heard him confess to it. After all, Borges had changed his version of the night of the killing several times until finally, given the lie detector test, he decided to come clean.

Shortly after Lyon had wound down his opening statement, I called my first witness, Lieutenant John Cashman. The only reason I wanted him first was to get into evidence a drawing of the layout of the interior of the Kralik house. It would support my argument that Barbara's killer must have been familiar with the house and where Barbara slept. It would also punch holes in any testimony from Moseley, whose description of the interior had been erroneous.

Next on the stand was Dr. David Rothstein, Marie Kralik's personal physician, who testified that she was too ill to appear. His testimony, while brief, couldn't help but draw sympathy to the plight of the Kralik family. Without objection by Lyon, Marie's testimony at the first trial was admitted in evidence, and I read it in full to the jurors, in the process introducing eleven photographs of the crime scene taken by police photographers to support Cashman's layout of the house.

Dr. James Kurian, a surgical resident at Queens General Hospital, who had pronounced Barbara dead, appeared next, followed by Dr. Richard Grimes, the medical examiner who had performed Barbara's autopsy. His testimony was important, because he detailed the horrific nature of the wounds, to the chest five to six inches deep and to the abdomen four to five inches deep. I glanced at the jurors to gauge the impact of this testimony on them. Some of them were clearly unable to mask their horror; the monstrous nature of the attack had been clearly established.

Through Dr. Grimes, I was able to establish that the scissors Mitchell had stolen from the school could have produced wounds of the type that had killed Barbara Kralik. "Doctor," I said, "I show you these scissors, People's exhibit 13, for identification, and I ask you if scissors of this type could have produced the wounds you observed on the body of Barbara Kralik?"

"Yes, I believe so," he readily answered.

Good, I thought when Dr. Grimes was finished. His testimony supported the argument of intent to kill, an essential element necessary for a conviction of murder in the second degree.

Next, I called Joseph Kralik to the stand. As he approached the witness stand, hunched over, all eyes in the room were on him. In the first trial it had been difficult for him to disguise his anger, and I hoped this time he would clamp it down. As he spoke of events in the Kralik home on the night of the murder, my fears were put to rest. Instead of being angry, Joseph appeared overcome by grief, an impression that grew more pronounced toward the end of my questioning.

Required to prove that Barbara's dead body had been identified, I ended my questioning of Joseph by asking, "And did you on the morning of July 21, identify the dead body of your daughter Barbara Kralik to Dr. Grimes, the medical examiner?"

"Yes, sir," he answered, about to break down.

"Was the body that you observed in Queensboro Mortuary on July 21 the dead body of your daughter Barbara Kralik?"

"Yes, sir," he answered again, and then completely fell apart, tears streaming down his face.

While it wasn't a reaction I had anticipated, it certainly had an effect on the jurors, some of whom had their heads bowed in sympathy. Lyon, taken back, asked for a recess and offered to delay cross-examination.

"I wouldn't want to ask him a question right now, Your Honor," the defense attorney explained.

But Kralik didn't need a delay. "You can ask me," he piped up, wiping his eyes.

Kralik owned two boats, and Lyon's cross was limited to questions concerning their location on the night of the murder, in the water or alongside the house. The boats were a non-issue. Lyon should have skipped over the cross altogether. By going ahead with it, he merely prolonged the time the distraught Kralik was on the stand in sight of sympathetic jurors.

It was George Borges's turn next. With nervous anxiety, because I never knew what would come out of his mouth, I called him to the witness stand. He had the same cocky swagger I had seen in the first trial; apparently his scrapes with the law hadn't humbled him. Having changed his version of the night of July 19 through the morning of July 20 several times and having lied to Bernard Patten, Herbert Lyon, his attorneys, his own mother and me, he was the weakest link in the prosecution case—and a defense attorney's dream witness. Unfortunately, I had to call him as a witness. He was the only person I had who could actually place Mitchell in the Kralik house at the time of the attack. If I were lucky, he would testify to having dropped Mitchell off at a bus stop on Springfield Boulevard. This would be corroborated by the testimony of James Lewis, and the jurors would believe him. If I weren't so fortunate, the jurors would believe the police had coerced Borges. If he'd been forced into making false statements, they might reason, Mitchell could have been too.

I kept the direct examination as short as possible. Borges recounted driving Mitchell to the Kralik house and seeing him come "running out maybe fifteen minutes later. He told me, Let's go. I asked him what happened, so I started, you know, I started driving. He told me he stabbed this girl or a girl."

In an attempt to minimize the damage Lyon would do on cross-examination, I disclosed the inconsistent statements previously made by Borges, hoping to establish, nonetheless, that his testimony in this trial was the truth.

Lyon's cross-examination of Borges was what I expected, devastatingly biting and effective. He brought out every previous statement in which Borges denied driving Mitchell to the Kralik house. Judge Thompson gave Lyon great latitude in this area and repeatedly denied my objections to the repetitious questioning. The cross dragged on, consuming the entire afternoon and extending into the following day, a Friday.

Lyon pressed Borges relentlessly about why he had changed his testimony. Was it because ADA Patten and I had promised him a lenient sentence for the school burglary?

"No," Borges answered, "they didn't tell me nothing about it...I asked the DA, and he didn't say anything. 'It's up to the Judge, the sentencing Judge.'" As far as I knew, no promises had been made to Borges or his attorney by anyone in the DA's office or the sentencing judge.

I approached the witness stand for the redirect. Unlike Lyon, I knew the real reason for Borges's final change of testimony, and I was going to bring it out now, because of the explosive effect it would have. Good thing it was Friday afternoon and there was a three-day weekend coming up, I thought—the jurors will have time to absorb it.

"Before the last trial, George, I came down to the Brooklyn Youth House with Mr. Patten to talk to you. Is that correct?" I asked.

"Yes," he said without hesitation, looking at the jurors.

"And did you lie to me when I asked you for the truth at that time?"

"Yes."

"Thereafter did you change your mind and decide to tell the truth?"

"Yes."

"Why, George?"

"You gave me a lie detector test."

I glanced at the jurors. Clearly, they registered the remark, some leaning forward, listening intently.

Lyon, visibly shaken, jumped to his feet, and without even objecting blurted out, "Alright, now I move for a mistrial."

Thompson promptly denied Lyon's motion, to which Lyon took exception.

When Lyon finished his second cross-examination of Borges, Judge Thompson recessed the court until Monday, then summoned Lyon and me to his chambers.

"I want to discuss the lie detector answer," Thompson said.

"New York law prohibits offering in evidence the results of a polygraph test and is therefore inadmissible," Lyon said.

Judge Thompson stared at me. "Your Honor," I responded, "the results of the test have not been mentioned. It was Lyon's extensive cross-examination of Borges about why he changed his mind that prompted me to ask for the reason he decided to tell the truth."

"I'm willing to give Mr. Lyon an opportunity to submit a memorandum of law on the subject," the judge said. "Perhaps that will change my mind. In the meantime I'll permit the DA to submit a memorandum of law as well. On Tuesday, if my ruling remains the same, Mr. Lyon, you can have further cross-examination of Borges related to the polygraph."

That evening, after consulting with Frank O'Connor, I briefed Ben Jacobson, chief of the Appeals Bureau in the DA's office, on the legal issue that had erupted over the lie detector test. Jacobson said he would have a memorandum of law for me first thing Tuesday morning.

"You had a right to ask why the witness decided to tell the truth," he reassured me. "It will stand up on appeal, I promise you."

I was looking forward to the three-day holiday and hoping to spend some time with my children with just minimal trial-related work. On Saturday morning, I called James Lewis, the bus driver, and informed him that his testimony would probably start on the following Tuesday, February 23.

"How do you feel?" I said. "Are you comfortable with what you're going to say?"

"I'm okay with it. You made everything clear to me about being one hundred percent positive. I am, and I'm not afraid to get up there and testify."

This conversation relaxed me, and I was able to spend the first quality time in over eight months with Beth, Robert, and Caren. Still, in the back of my mind the image of Barbara Kralik lurked, and as I played with the kids, I couldn't help but think of the pain her parents were feeling as a result of her loss. I needed to get a conviction. It was the only solace left for that poor family.

Ben Jacobson faithfully carried out his promise to prepare the memorandum. Instead of waiting until Tuesday, he delivered it personally to my home on Monday night. It was helpful to have it earlier than expected, not least because it was exhaustive on the subject of polygraph tests, with references to the law in a number of states, not just New York.

Ben had taken a surprising approach to the question of polygraphs in general. Instead of stating our position by referring to the issue of the admissibility of test results, he first argued that the court could, under proper circumstances, consider their admissibility. Though at the time the case law of New York was heavily weighted against admissibility, the New York Court of Appeals hadn't yet reviewed any case that had gone into the scientific foundation for polygraph examinations. However, if the court did review one, it could rule otherwise if sufficient scientific evidence supported their reliability. In this case, Ben argued—and this supported Judge Thompson's initial ruling on the subject—there was no need to hear any scientific evidence, as the test results had not been offered in evidence in the first place.

After reading over the memorandum, I called Ben. "The Mitchell case isn't the forum for creating broad law on the admissibility of a polygraph test. I'll rely on any inferences the jury is willing to draw about Borges's answer to the question that he decided to tell the truth because of the test." Ben agreed with me.

First thing Tuesday morning, the two memoranda of law, Lyon's and Jacobson's, were submitted to Judge Thompson in court. Lyon based his position on the New York rule of inadmissibility, the same argument he'd made on Friday. There was nothing fresh in it. It enabled me to argue that Lyon was taking a position that wasn't relevant to the issue. I wasn't offering the polygraph test at all and wouldn't offer it, unless Lyon consented to it going into evidence. Although the jury hadn't yet appeared, I made the last statement for the benefit of the media, so that they would infer that the test established that Borges lied when he denied driving Mitchell to the Kralik house and hearing him admit the attack.

In the end, Judge Thompson dismissed Lyon's request for a mistrial but permitted further cross-examination of Borges. The defense attorney fired off a few questions about the circumstances surrounding the test, without going into its results, then revisited certain questions he'd posed before the weekend break. Judge Thompson gave Lyon leeway, allowing him to proceed over my objections. The further cross availed Lyon nothing.

CHAPTER SIXTEEN

"Next witness!" Judge Thompson said.

"James Lewis," I called out in a ringing voice.

The defense team and all the reporters turned toward the rear of the courtroom, stretching their necks. Lewis was a name that hadn't surfaced in the previous trial, a name I'd revealed when announcing my anticipated witnesses at the start of jury selection before Judge Thompson.

Although Lyon may have learned of Lewis's existence before the trial, he couldn't possibly have foreseen what sort of witness the man would turn out to be. As Lewis made his debut, dressed in a dark suit, white shirt, and tie, he appeared calm and distinguished. Rather than dictating what to wear, I had merely suggested that he not show up in casual clothes. All eyes followed him as he proceeded, tall and erect, down the aisle of the packed courtroom to the witness box, passing between the counsel tables and glancing at Mitchell. After taking the oath, he sat down, seemingly unfazed by the spotlight.

My direct examination would be short and swift, without any conflict between my questions and Lewis's answers. Lyon was sure to go after Lewis on cross-examination, attacking his memory and his failure to come forward before the first trial. But he would have to handle this witness gently, with kid gloves, so as not to appear to be badgering him.

After all, Lewis was what lawyers call a disinterested witness—he had no personal interest in the outcome of the case.

Though my heart was pounding—all the hopes for the truth that I'd harbored for ten grueling months were pinned on this man's statements—I approached the witness stand with confidence. Unlike the mercurial George Borges, James Lewis was rock solid.

"Mr. Lewis, would you state your occupation, sir?"

"I am a bus driver for the New York City Transit Authority."

Out of the corner of my eye, I could see the defense team scribbling away. Caught off guard by this new witness, Lyon and his associates would have to make detailed notes of every word out of Lewis's mouth if they hoped to make any headway on cross-examination.

At my request, Judge Thompson directed Mitchell to stand, and he was identified for the record as the defendant.

"Have you ever seen Alvin Mitchell before?" I asked Lewis.

"Yes I have." Lewis said he'd seen Mitchell on the morning of July 20, 1963, at approximately 4:15 a.m. "As I came to the corner of Springfield and North Conduit, I saw a young man at this corner leaning against a pole. Now, I didn't know at this time whether he wanted the bus or not, so I completed turning around the corner. I was making a right turn off of Conduit into Springfield, and as I came alongside of him he pushed himself off of the pole and showed intentions that he wanted the bus, so I stopped there, and as he started up the steps I noticed that he was staggering a bit, as if he was intoxicated. He came up to the bar by the fare box, and he gave me a dollar bill, and I noticed that the hand with which he handed me the dollar bill had a white handkerchief around it, and there was blood stains on it. I gave him the change…and he took the change in the hand with the…handkerchief around it, and [with his left hand] took out fifteen cents and dropped it into the fare box. At this point he staggered back against the bar, and his head dropped down, and his hair fell over his face. He took his left hand and pushed his hair back, and then he proceeded to the rear of the bus."

"Did you observe how he was dressed?"

"Yes, I did."

"Would you tell the jury how he was dressed?"

"He had on a black T-shirt and a black pair of pants."

"Can you describe the weather conditions when you first observed the defendant, Alvin Mitchell, that night?"

"It was a rainy night. It had been raining most of the night, and at this time the streets were very wet. And one thing that makes me so sure of that is that this corner is very dangerous and slippery when it's wet, and I had to proceed…with great caution, otherwise the bus would skid forward instead of…making the right turn. And this is the way that I noticed him, because on a normal turn I swing out, and I would probably have not seen him at that pole at the time."

"Subsequent to the time that he went to the back of the bus, after depositing the money, did you observe him again?"

"Yes, about five minutes later. I was making a right turn at 140th Avenue and Farmers Boulevard. There is also a pole on that corner…you have to be careful in checking the clearance around there, otherwise you might hit the pole with the rear of the bus when you're turning. So I checked the…rearview mirror that is inside of the bus to see if I could see the pole, to tell how close I was at the rear of the bus, and at this point I noticed Mitchell's head sort of hanging out of the rear window on the right side of the bus."

I asked Lewis, "This is 140th and Farmers Boulevard, is that correct?"

"That is correct," he quickly answered.

The location of 140th and Farmers Boulevard was critical, because it was only one block from the Kralik house. Mitchell certainly would have wanted to see or hear anything going on in the vicinity.

I concluded my direct examination of Lewis with his testimony about the event in his life that he associated with the night in question: bringing the newspapers to his wife in the hospital on Sunday, July 21, 1963, two days after his daughter was born.

"In glancing through them I noticed the article about the death of the girl," Lewis said.

The jurors appeared to be hanging on Lewis's every word, and the whispering from the spectators' seats turned into a noticeable buzz. I thought Judge Thompson was going to gavel the courtroom for silence, but he didn't.

After a five-minute recess, Lyon began his assault.

"Which route did you take in September of 1959?" he asked Lewis.

Without hesitation, as he would throughout his testimony, Lewis answered, "In September of 1959, I was working out of the East New York depot in Brooklyn."

"Where did you go?"

"They had several lines there."

"Name one."

"The B-56."

"Where did that go from, where to where?"

"It was from East New York and Fulton Street to 171st Street and Jamaica Avenue."

"What other lines?"

"Well, there was the B-12, the East New York line."

"Where did that go?"

"From Crescent Street and Liberty Avenue to Prospect Park at Ocean Avenue."

Lyon's attempt to impugn the witness quickly foundered. In addition to being thoroughly familiar with his own routes, Lewis was able to detail the complete route of another line that he hadn't driven in over four years and name the exact dates and years on which he'd been transferred from one depot to another.

Later in the cross-examination, Lyon asked Lewis where he'd been on August 29, 1963. This was the day following Mitchell's confession and his arrest for the murder of Barbara Kralik. It was a date that had no special connection to Lewis's life, yet the witness immediately answered that he wasn't working, because it was his day off.

"You were off?" Lyon pressed.

"Right."

"What day of the week was August 29?"

"Thursday."

"Are you sure of that?"

"Right."

Lewis was a perfect prosecution witness. He was so effective and believable that at one point during the cross-examination, Lyon actually confessed, "Your Honor, I'm a little shaken up."

I scanned the jurors' faces as Lyon pressed Lewis in an attempt to test his memory and credibility. But Lewis's memory was uncannily sharp and devastating to the defense. Some of the jurors smiled with each quick and positive answer Lewis made to Lyon's probing questions. I sensed that these jurors were glad Lyon was getting nowhere in his effort to break Lewis down. When his testimony ended, I was sure of one thing, Mitchell wasn't going to be acquitted. There might be another hung jury, but now there was also a realistic chance that he would be held responsible for the killing of Barbara Kralik.

Only a few minutes remained before Judge Thompson recessed the trial for the day. I wanted my first police witness to have a positive impact on the jury with straightforward testimony. And so I called Charles Prasse to the stand.

This twenty-two-year veteran of the police force had been carefully chosen by Dowd to be a member of the Kralik task force. Prasse was assigned, along with his partner, Detective Stankus, to check out Mitchell's various statements about how he got home in the period from the night of July 19 into the morning of July 20. Like all my key police witnesses, he had already testified three times in this case, twice before Judge Shapiro and once in the voluntariness hearing in this trial. Prasse described his participation in the police investigation chronologically, emphasizing the limited number of days—six over a six-week period —that detectives had questioned Mitchell. Calmly, succinctly, and without hesitation, Prasse testified to the changing versions Mitchell had given the detectives about his actions and how he got home. Unfortunately, before I had completed my direct examination, Judge Thompson recessed the trial until the following morning.

As I was leaving the courtroom, Jack Peters handed me a note that the Chief wanted to see me.

"How did Lewis's testimony go in?" O'Connor asked almost as soon as I set foot in his office.

"Without a hitch," I answered. "He was an incredible witness, with an even more impressive memory than I expected. When I get the minutes of his testimony tomorrow morning, I'll have Jack copy it for you to read. It should ease your mind in case you have any lingering doubt about Mitchell's guilt."

O'Connor replied, "Charlie, it isn't a question of lingering doubt. For me, the Balestrero case has and always will be a guideline when there is any question of a person's guilt. I've been reading all the newspaper articles that infer Mitchell's innocence. How do I get around that?"

The Balestrero case, in which O'Connor was the defense counsel, would always be his yardstick of the danger of mistaken identity. It was one in which Emanuel Balestrero was wrongly identified by no less than five people as having committed a robbery.

"Chief, this isn't the Balestrero case. It isn't a case of mistaken identity. The issue is whose confession is true: the defendant's or a convicted murderer's? The papers may be reacting this way to make amends for the way they came down on Mitchell when he was first arrested. I have absolutely no doubt that Mitchell killed the girl. But I wasn't a witness. Neither was Lyon. In the end, it's for the jury to decide what the truth is. You've been more than fair in this case. If you hadn't granted Moseley immunity from prosecution for killing Barbara Kralik, he never would have testified in the first trial. We're going to do it again in this trial."

"I guess that's a good way to look at it," O'Connor said. "Send me Lewis's testimony as soon as you get it."

When the trial resumed the next morning, Judge Thompson delayed my direct questioning of Prasse to permit Lyon to conduct additional cross-examination of George Borges related to the polygraph examination. I handed Lyon the report of the polygraph examination, but he avoided any reference to its contents. I didn't even request that it be entered into evidence, knowing Lyon would have none of that.

In an attempt to discredit Borges, Lyon revisited questions from his earlier cross-examination of the witness. Although nothing new surfaced,

Lyon appeared to be making some headway, fueled by the inconsistent testimony. I objected numerous times to no avail. Then finally Judge Thompson put an end to the interrogation and excused Borges from the witness stand. A major difference between Lyon's approach during his examination of witnesses and mine began to emerge. Newspaper articles had clearly been hostile to Borges, and it dawned on me that when Lyon made a telling point that seemed to benefit his client, he would glance in the direction of the reporters, all seated in the first two spectator rows. I was trying my case for the jurors, while Lyon was trying his case for the media in hopes that their reporting would influence the jury. Although Judge Thompson had instructed the jury, which wasn't sequestered, not to read newspaper articles or watch television news about the trial, there was no guarantee that his order was being followed.

It was unsettling, but I made up my mind not to be affected or distracted by anything the media said or wrote. I had to keep my eyes on my goal: exposing the truth.

When my direct examination of Prasse resumed, I concentrated on having him justify the intervals between the days of Mitchell's questioning. Prasse described how he and the other detectives had checked each of the differing stories the defendant had served up to explain how he'd made it home on the night of the murder. The detectives questioned Mitchell's neighbors, asking if anyone owned a green Rambler, the model he had said was the one that had given him a lift. In another version of his story, Mitchell claimed to have received a ride from a stranger delivering a package to an Astoria Movie Theater. Following up, the detectives visited every movie theater in Astoria and the surrounding areas. In yet another version, Mitchell said he got a ride home from a man with whom he discussed bareback riding at one of the horse academies on Long Island. The detectives went to every riding academy on Long Island without confirming this tale. Surely, I thought, the jury would see these follow-up efforts as honest attempts to get at the truth.

I knew from my trial preparation of Prasse that Lyon would have problems cross-examining him.

"Now, in the questioning of Alvin Mitchell, did you ever threaten him in any way?" Lyon asked.

"No, I did not," Prasse replied.

"Did you ever accuse him of lying?"

"I may have implied he was lying."

"Just implied it. Is that what you're saying, sir?"

"I can't be certain that I used the word *lie*."

"Well, did you avoid using the word *lie*?"

"Very likely I didn't specifically try to avoid using the word *lie*."

"But you don't think you used the word *lie*."

"It's hard for me to say. I may have used it."

"Well, tell me, sir, were you...just as polite in questioning Alvin Mitchell as you are on the stand today?"

"I don't remember saying 'yes, sir' to him, if that's what you call politeness."

"Well, were you just as quiet spoken and as deliberate with your speech as you are today when you spoke to Alvin Mitchell?"

"I would say my voice may have raised or lowered at times."

"It's a different situation, isn't it, in a police station?"

"There is a lot more noise in a police station."

"And the whole atmosphere is a little different, isn't it?"

"The atmosphere is different, yes."

Lyon got nowhere.

My next witness was Detective Leon Stankus, Prasse's partner of several years. A police officer for nine years, he had been promoted to detective after only a year on the force as a result of heroism. Well over six feet tall, he was an imposing figure, which must have come in handy when questioning a suspect. Of all the police officers I anticipated calling, he was the one I believed Lyon would make his strongest effort to break on cross-examination, because during Borges's testimony, he had identified Stankus as having physically abused and threatened him. If Stankus's testimony went in without Lyon scoring any significant points, then the defense attorney's argument that Mitchell's confession was involuntary would be seriously weakened.

Although not as articulate as Prasse, Detective Stankus turned out to be almost as effective in detailing the different stories Mitchell had told the detectives during questioning, and my concern that this witness might leave holes in the police testimony quickly ebbed.

During a short cross-examination of Stankus, Lyon, in an unsuccessful effort to discredit him, introduced a DD5, a supplemental report the detective had prepared following Mitchell's questioning on August 9, 1963. Bingo! I thought. Had this report not gone into evidence, the jurors would have had to rely on their memory of the different stories the detectives testified Mitchell had told them. Now they could take the DD5 into the jury room during deliberations.

When Lyon ended his cross, I asked the court for permission to read this exhibit to the jury, and it was granted. Facing the jury box, I began in a slow, deliberate voice so as to emphasize the contents. "Subject stated when first questioned the same details as he had given on previous interviews, with the exception that the unknown person who had given him a lift from Flushing to Astoria was a male, white, approximately thirty years, five foot ten, about 200 pounds. This unknown person was driving a 1963 Rambler, green, two door. This person told him that he goes bareback horseback riding at some riding academy out on Long Island…Subject, after being continuously questioned changed his story to the following: He stated that all he had said on previous interviews about Friday night…were stories that he had made up. Subject stated that the truth is that he couldn't remember what happened Friday night after he had left George to go back to the school to get his shirt. Subject stated that he couldn't remember if he found his shirt or if he did go back to the school to get it. Subject stated that all that he could remember after he had left George was that he was going back to the school for his shirt, that he next remembers getting off a bus in Jamaica and walking to a subway station. Subject states that he couldn't recall if this bus was coming from Flushing or from Springfield Gardens."

That was a key point. Raising my eyes, I could see the jurors leaning forward in their seats, absorbing what I was reading. Then I continued reading: "Subject states that the next thing he could remember was that he was walking on Steinway Street near his home in Astoria. Subject then states that he does not remember how he entered his home or how he went to bed. He does not recall whether or not he had a shirt when he got home. He does recall that upon awakening he gave his mother a pair of scissors, also recalls that he told his mother that he got home [at] 12:30 a.m. He recalls that when his mother asked him about the cut on his wrist, he told her that some boys pushed him while on his way home, against a sharp object...When questioning of Mitchell resumed, he stated that what he had previously said about not being able to remember what happened Friday night, after he and Borges broke into the school in Flushing, was all not true. At this time he stated that he did remember all that happened, even though he was drinking heavily. The purpose of his saying that he couldn't remember, he said, was that he felt that that story would be believed. Subject after further questioning reverted back to his original story."

As soon as I finished reading the DD5, Judge Thompson recessed the trial until the following morning. The break couldn't have come at a more opportune time. Without any additional testimony to clutter their minds, the jurors could go home mulling over the contents of the DD5, and I hoped that, as a result, its significance would sink in—that the defendant's different versions to the detectives about how he got home were designed to cover up the truth. This, added to the details from the bus driver's testimony, could help the jurors find the truth, I hoped.

I made a note to myself to emphasize, during the summation, that the police hadn't known anything about Lewis when questioning Mitchell and Borges in July and August of 1963.

Expecting the prosecution case to wind up within the next two days, I was starting to see a little light at the end of the tunnel. The end of the prosecution case would take the pressure off me, since questioning on direct examination was more restrictive than cross-examining defense witnesses.

Still, there were plenty of potential land mines ahead. Any significant flaws in my remaining witnesses' testimony could poke holes in the entire police investigation and make it almost impossible to get certain exhibits into evidence, including the critical confession to Jim Burnes filmed by ABC-TV.

Detective John Palmer, my next witness, was important, because I needed to get into evidence the written copy of questions and answers from his interrogation of Mitchell. I also hoped to get into evidence written questions and answers from Palmer's interview with George Borges.

During my direct examination, Palmer told what he had seen in the Kralik house when he arrived in the early morning hours of July 20. Barbara was just being put into the ambulance, and Palmer directed his partner, Detective Fullam, to stay with her in an effort to find out what had happened.

As his testimony proceeded, Palmer said that it was in the early morning hours of August 29 when he'd first questioned Mitchell and wrote down the answers verbatim. I asked the court if the Q&A could be entered into evidence, and permission was granted. Later, however, when I attempted to do the same with Palmer's handwritten copy of the interrogation of Borges, Judge Thompson refused to allow it.

As soon as Lyon started his cross-examination, he committed a faux pas. He was pressing Palmer to describe how Mitchell had pointed out the location of Barbara's bed during the reenactment of the crime.

"Did you tell him, 'Alvin, go home, come back five days later, I don't want you to lie, be absolutely sure, but if you can remember that you were ever in that bedroom before July 20, I'd like to know about it.'"

"That question is facetious," Judge Thompson piped up without skipping a beat. "Jury will disregard it. Quite obvious, Mr. Lyon, Palmer had said already that he had the defendant in custody. Defendant allegedly confessed to a crime. They certainly wouldn't send him home for five days."

There was one area that Lyon did pursue relentlessly, and I didn't object. Palmer had recovered a serrated knife one block from the Kralik house on the morning of July 20, and Lyon's cross-examination was designed to imply that this serrated knife could have been the murder weapon.

"Didn't you find a knife yourself?" Lyon asked.

"There was another knife that was found across the street from a house," answered Palmer, adding the location being a block from the Kralik house.

"And could you tell us how big it was and how long a blade?"

"It was a steak knife, a common kitchen knife, serrated edge to it, bone handle."

Moseley had testified in the first trial that he had stabbed Barbara Kralik with a serrated knife, and I expected him to do the same in this trial.

Knowing that Dr. Grimes had ruled out a serrated knife as a murder weapon, I immediately dispatched Jack Peters to phone Grimes and ask him to rush to the courthouse. As soon as he arrived, I would put Dr. Grimes on the stand, no matter who was testifying. None of Barbara's wounds showed any signs of having been inflicted by a serrated knife. This was a critical material discrepancy in Moseley's version of the homicide.

Captain Dowd was next on the witness stand. Lyon, I suspected, would have a more difficult time with him than with any other police officer. It wasn't only that Dowd was better educated or more experienced than any other police officer, or even that he was the leader of the task force. His gentle, almost serene nature coupled with an impeccable appearance made it almost impossible to find him untruthful.

In his testimony, Dowd clearly explained why days and even weeks passed between the interrogations of Mitchell. More than 130 detectives had investigated Barbara's killing, conducting between 750 and 800 interviews and interrogations. Everyone was suspect, even Joseph Kralik for a short time.

Before Lyon started his cross-examination of Captain Dowd, Dr. Grimes arrived. With the permission of the judge, I called him to the witness stand. I marked the serrated steak knife discovered a block from the Kralik house as an exhibit and showed it to the witness.

"Dr. Grimes, I show you People's exhibit 18 for identification, and I ask you to examine it. Have you seen People's exhibit 18 for identification before?"

"Yes, sir, I have."

"Now, Doctor, I ask you, could People's exhibit 18 for identification have produced the wounds you observed on the body of Barbara Kralik?"

"No, this knife could not produce the wounds which I described."

During Lyon's cross-examination of Dr. Grimes, the doctor clearly and carefully explained the absence of serrations to Barbara's wounds, which ruled out the knife as a murder weapon.

When Lyon was done with Grimes, he then began his cross-examination of Captain Dowd. It was thorough but not fruitful for the defense. In an attempt to trap Dowd into making inconsistent statements, Lyon posed questions that jumped from one interrogation of Alvin Mitchell to another, jumbling the chronological order. Dowd held his ground, and finally Judge Thompson put an end to the badgering, saying that the witness's statements "are not inconsistent with the witness's testimony." Thompson's intervention watered down whatever inferences Lyon was making about the accuracy or truthfulness of Captain Dowd's testimony.

Furthermore, Lyon again fell into a trap I had set. At the trial before Judge Shapiro, Dowd had testified to a palm print found in the Kralik house that hadn't been identified or compared with Winston Moseley's palm print. As I hoped, Lyon revisited this subject now, and Dowd said that the unidentified palm print had not been compared to Moseley's before the first trial.

On my redirect examination of Dowd, I sprang the trap: "Do you know that subsequent to the first trial I had Mr. Moseley's palm print compared with the palm print…found in the house?" I asked Dowd.

"Yes, sir."

"And do you know that Moseley's palm print has been excluded?"

"Yes, sir, I do know that."

Thus ended Dowd's testimony on a positive note for the prosecution. When the captain left the witness stand, Judge Thompson recessed the trial until the following morning, a Friday. I hoped to complete the prosecution case before the weekend started. Jim Burnes, the man who had filmed Alvin Mitchell's confession, would be my final witness. The timing was perfect. It would give jurors the entire weekend to absorb what I always considered the most important evidence in the entire case.

Back in my office, I received a phone call from Patten.

"As you requested," he informed me, "William Finn has been picked up by the police on arrest warrants charging him with being a major traffic scofflaw. He's being held on bail. How do you suggest I handle this?"

"I want him held in a cell adjoining the courtroom. In open court with the jury present, I'll tell Judge Thompson that he's next door, available to testify. If Lyon doesn't call him as a witness, I'll use that failure during my summation."

Late that night, a reporter called me at home. It came as no surprise. Several journalists had taken to calling me at the house, bombarding me with questions about how I felt the trial was going. I gave them all my standard line, that I wouldn't make any statements to the press until the trial was over. That is, until this particular reporter called.

"Do you really think Mitchell is guilty?" he wanted to know.

"If I had the slightest doubt of Mitchell's guilt, the case would have been dismissed before the first trial," I said. I still get a good laugh over that one. I couldn't imagine a more ridiculous question. Did the reporter actually believe I would prosecute someone I didn't think was guilty?

When I arrived in my office the following morning, Jim Burnes was waiting for me. Though I appreciated his promptness, I was disappointed to discover the reason for it.

"Can I testify first thing this morning?" Burnes said. "I'm going away for the weekend and want to get an early start."

I had no choice but to agree. So much for scheduling Burnes to appear at the tail end of Friday as the last witness for the prosecution. Shaking off the setback, I decided that in the end it wouldn't make a difference. In my summation, I would recommend that the jurors ask to see the film a second time, during deliberations.

Jack Peters, Jim Burnes, and I left a little early for the courtroom to set up the camera that ABC News had loaned me. Our office had its own camera, but ABC's had much better sound and a clearer picture. It was to be projected onto a five-by-five-foot screen purchased specifically for this trial. Owing to space restrictions, we had to angle the screen so that it partially faced the spectators, and although the jurors would have an unobstructed view of the screen, it was farther away from the jury box than I would have preferred. Should I ask Judge Thompson to permit the jurors to step out of the jury box and move closer to the screen? No. They could view it close up during deliberations if they chose to do so.

When the trial resumed, Lyon made a last-ditch effort to prevent the film from being introduced into evidence, making numerous objections on shaky legal grounds and consuming over half an hour. As the minutes slipped by, my hopes of completing the prosecution case before the end of the day diminished. At last Lyon finished his arguments, the judge overruled his objections to the film, and I called Jim Burnes to the stand.

Burnes's direct testimony was no different than in the first trial, and when it ended, I asked that the film be played for the jury, not once but several times. After Judge Thompson granted my request, the courtroom was darkened and in total silence. Not one sound could be heard, not even a whisper from the defense table or any reporter. I could see the jurors staring at the screen even before the film started to roll. I moved off to the side, standing close enough to the jurors to get a good view of their faces. They leaned forward in anticipation. As the film rolled, Mitchell could be easily identified, dressed in jeans and a polo shirt and appearing calm. With only the flickering light from the film, I strained to search the jurors' faces and saw looks of amazement. It proved the old saying about a picture being worth a thousand words. There he was, the killer of a fifteen-year-old girl, a friend, admitting his crime before the whole world and, more importantly, to this jury.

"Why did you do it?" Burnes asked.

"I didn't mean to kill her. I don't remember stabbing her," Mitchell answered.

"Did you think you'd get caught?"

"I wanted to tell them from the beginning, but I was scared."

"Do you think you should be punished for it?"

"Yes."

"What form of punishment?"

"I don't know."

Lyon's cross-examination did little to test Burnes's testimony or lessen the impact of the film.

"Is it a fact that Alvin Mitchell looked pale during that interview?" Lyon said.

"I believe that he did," Burnes replied

"And nervous?"

"Slightly nervous, yes."

My redirect examination of Burnes was short and to the point.

"Mr. Burnes, did you observe the physical appearance of Mitchell?" I asked.

"Yes, I did."

"Did you see any marks or bruises on his person, sir?"

"I did not."

My final witness was Stanley Pryor, chief of the Criminal Court Bureau. Stanley was a no nonsense prosecutor whose bureau handled arraignments and hearings for all people charged with crimes in Queens County, as well as trials for misdemeanors. Both rigid and practical, he was inclined, in a weak case, to grant a plea reduction, but in a strong case where violence was involved he wouldn't consider it. Bright, streetwise, and a stickler for the truth, Pryor wasn't a person who could easily have the wool pulled over his eyes. There was no way he would have been part of a police conspiracy to obtain a false confession from Mitchell. It was Pryor's honesty that had helped convince me originally that Mitchell had killed Barbara Kralik.

Pryor was what many trial attorneys would call a professional witness, which made him all the more valuable to the prosecution. Like James Lewis, he had an excellent memory, and because the Mitchell case was the only investigation he had handled as an assistant District Attorney, his recollection wouldn't be muddied by the details of other investigations.

Pryor painted a clear, immutable picture of his conversations with Mitchell in the precinct during the early morning hours of August 29, 1963, when he first questioned him and took signed statements. Before the police stenographer arrived for a Q&A, Pryor questioned Mitchell orally, and his recall of this session was quite impressive: "I asked him if he knew where he was. He said yes...the 103ᵈ Squad Precinct...I asked him why he was there, and he told me he was there, because he killed Barbara Kralik...I told him I had previously learned that on five or six other occasions...he had made statements to the policemen that were untrue. I told him that I was going to ask a stenographer to appear at the station house and take stenographic minutes of the questions asked of him and the answers made by him...I asked him if he wanted me to call anyone. He said no...I asked him if he wanted me to call his folks. He said no. I asked him if he wanted any coffee. He said yes...I told one of the detectives in the squad room to go out and buy coffee, cigarettes, and Danish pastry.

"I then started asking Alvin questions...I asked him if he was telling me the truth voluntarily. He said yes. I asked him whether or not he was beaten or forced to make this statement by anyone. He said no. I said, 'Alvin, do you know Barbara?' He said yes. 'How long have you known her?' And he answered, 'Approximately a year and a half to two years.'

"'Do you know where she lives?' He said he didn't know the house address, but he knew the house. I asked him to describe the house for me. He told me it was a one-family house with two floors. I asked him if he had ever been in the house. He said yes...I asked him where the bathroom was located. He told me on the second floor.

"I asked him if he had ever gone out with Barbara Kralik. He said no, he had not. He said on one occasion he had a date to go out with a girl by the name of Pat Farfone. That was to be the christening of his brother's child. Pat wouldn't go with Alvin unless Barbara Kralik accompanied her. Pat didn't go to the christening, but since he had promised to take Barbara Kralik, he took her with him. I asked him if he ever went out with her on another date, and he said no...I asked him if he spoke to Pat. He said yes...approximately three times a week...he would see her, either by the candy store or the steps of her home.

"I asked him what day this had occurred, this incident for which he was in the station house. He said it occurred on July 20. I said, 'What time did it happen?' He said, 'Approximately four o'clock or ten minutes after four'...I asked him, 'How did it happen?' He said he stabbed her.

"I said, 'How did you get into the house?' He said he went through a window...grabbed hold of the windowsill and boosted himself into the room. I asked him what room he entered. He said the porch. I said, 'Where did you go from there?' He said, 'I went into the living room and then up the stairs up to Barbara Kralik's room.' I asked him whether or not anyone was in the room besides Barbara. He said he thought when he entered the room that there were two people sleeping in the bed, Pat Farfone and Barbara. He said he had motioned to or touched Pat to wake up, and at that time Barbara had awakened, screamed. He got scared. He then struck Barbara Kralik with a pair of scissors...

"He...said he got panicky...ran out of the house through the side entrance on the first floor, ran to the rear of the house, ran around the corner of the back of the house, out to the hedge. At the hedge, he tripped over a fence that was hidden from view...and fell down, picked himself up, ran to the corner to the car, and George Borges was in the car. He told George Borges, 'Get the hell out of here fast. I've just killed a girl.' And they drove away. [He said] that somewhere in the travels of going down the road, he threw away the scissors. I asked him if he knew where he threw away the scissors. He said he knew the approximate location. I asked him why he had gone into Barbara Kralik's house that morning, and he told me he thought he would try to lay Pat Farfone. I asked him whether or not he had ever done it before. He said he had not...I believe that those were the questions I put to him at that particular time."

Pryor went on and on, without my interrupting, making eye contact with the jurors to emphasize important parts of his testimony. He testified that immediately after the oral questioning, he had conducted a formal Q&A with the steno present, which was typed up and then signed by Mitchell. The confession basically followed the lines of the oral questioning, with the same answers. Judge Thompson received the Q&A in evidence, and after reading it to the jurors, I let them pass it around and glance at the contents. It was important that each juror see the typewritten confession with Mitchell's signature on the bottom of each page, something they would never see from Winston Moseley, because no such signed document existed.

Lyon's cross-examination of Pryor consumed the rest of the afternoon, but for whatever reason, it was less pressing than it had been in the first trial and the hearing.

When it was done, I breathed a sigh of relief, having managed after all to wind up my case before the weekend recess. It was of immeasurable strategic value. While Judge Thompson instructed the jury to keep an open mind and not form any opinions, the jurors, being human, would be impressed by what they saw and heard on this last day of the prosecution case, and there were two whole days for it to sink in.

After Judge Thompson sent the jurors home, Lyon made a motion to dismiss the prosecution case. It was promptly denied by the judge.

"I know you've broken your back on these trials," Frank O'Connor said during our daily chat, "but you must understand that the Mitchell case can't go on and on. I've decided that if there is no verdict in this trial, there won't be a third trial. My mind is made up. I'm telling you now instead of at the end of the trial in the hope it will give you additional incentive to win."

What O'Connor said wasn't particularly surprising other than for its timing. After all, before Cacciatore, Patten, and I talked him into it, he'd been opposed to the second trial.

I made one last stab at changing his mind. "What a shame it would be if Mitchell gets away with this murder, because an animal like Moseley confessed to Barbara's murder to set up a defense of insanity. I'll tell you something nobody seems to remember or think about. Mitchell never *once* denied killing Barbara from the time he first confessed on August 29, 1963, until after Moseley was arrested in March of 1964, more than six months later. If Mitchell had been tried before Moseley was arrested, he probably would have been quickly convicted. Now all Lyon needs is one juror to hold out for acquittal, and it's the ball game, Mitchell walks free. At least we'll still have him for the school burglary."

"True," O'Connor said. "If he's acquitted, or there's a hung jury, I intend to personally appear before the sentencing judge and ask the maximum sentence be imposed on the burglary charge. So no matter what happens, he doesn't walk."

Before leaving the office that evening, I made one last phone call, to Moseley's attorney, Sidney Sparrow. Did he have any idea how his client was going to testify? The answer was a swift no.

CHAPTER SEVENTEEN

Jack Peters and I spent Saturday and Sunday preparing for the defense witnesses, concentrating on three: Mitchell, Winston Moseley, and William Finn. We had collated the minutes of the first trial with cue cards, each card a separate outline of a specific area for cross-examining a witness and on which we included the page numbers of each witness's prior testimony. In case previous testimony differed from testimony during this trial, it could easily be located and used to contradict the witness.

I expected nothing new in the way of Mitchell's testimony. Surely Lyon and his staff had prepared him carefully by repeatedly reviewing his prior testimony. I intended to be guided by my cross-examination in the first trial, with two exceptions. First, I was going to vary the order of my questioning; instead of proceeding chronologically, I planned to jump from one subject to another, mixing up time and place. Second, I would have to connect Mitchell to the newly presented testimony of bus driver James Lewis. I decided to emphasize Mitchell's statement, not prompted by any police officer, that he went home by bus and train, as well as his stated travel route. I would also question Mitchell about whether he had ever hitched a ride home from Springfield Gardens and, if so, from where. It was possible that in my summation I could argue he'd been trying to hitch a ride at 4:15 a.m. on July 20 when Lewis's bus came along, and he got on it. This would bolster Lewis's testimony.

My cue cards for Winston Moseley were limited to the discrepancies between his description of the crime and the uncontested facts. I had decided not to conduct an extensive cross-examination of him, convinced it would be a blunder more likely to reinforce his claim to having killed Barbara Kralik. I was planning to limit my cross to no more than fifteen minutes, assuming no interruptions from Lyon or Judge Thompson. Dispensing of him quickly was a way of dismissing him and diminishing his significance. Very quickly, I hoped, the jurors would see that Moseley was far off target and couldn't possibly have killed Barbara.

As for William Finn, I fervently hoped Lyon would call him as a witness, because if the jury believed Finn was lying when he said he gave Mitchell a ride home, they would also believe Mitchell was lying when he said Finn gave him that ride. Furthermore, if any witness willfully testified falsely to any material fact, the jury was allowed by law to disregard the entire testimony if they deemed fit. Knowing how risky it would be for Lyon to call Finn as a witness, I prepared a special cue card to be read in front of the jury in case he wasn't summoned. It read: "I've produced William Finn by court order, and he's available to testify for the defense. He's next door."

On Monday morning, the corridor outside the courtroom was pure bedlam, and it was only by some miracle that Jack and I managed to push our gurney through the crowd. "When will Moseley be testifying?" one of the court buffs shouted. I shrugged and said, "Your guess is as good as mine." So that's the reason the crowd has grown, I thought, morbid curiosity.

The number of journalists had more than doubled since Friday. Let into the room before general spectators, they filled three rows on both sides of the aisle. Anything related to Kitty Genovese and Winston Moseley always sold newspapers. When the doors opened and the general herd trampled in, they headed first for the seats on the right side of the courtroom, which provided an almost unobstructed view of the witness stand.

As soon as Judge Thompson convened the court, Lyon called his first defense witness: William Mitchell. The defendant's father testified that he'd been awakened from sleep when his son entered the house on the night of July 19 and that it was still dark, though he didn't know what time it was. He said his son had been held back several times in school and removed altogether at the age of sixteen. Sent upstate to live with an uncle and seek work, Mitchell returned to New York City in 1962 when the family moved from Springfield Gardens to Astoria, and the defendant obtained employment with the Welsbach Corporation as a packer and cargo handler. His direct testimony included a discussion of the black T-shirt allegedly worn by his son on the night of Barbara's murder.

"Had any of the clothes been washed at that time?" Lyon asked.

"No, nothing has been washed."

"And where did Detective Stankus take the clothes from?"

"There was a pile in our living room, a big pile, and he dug through it, and he took a shirt."

"What kind of shirt?"

"A black shirt."

"Was it a black T-shirt?"

"Yes."

This contradicted what the police officers had told me—that the shirt appeared to have been cleaned. Previously received in evidence by Judge Thompson, the shirt was absolutely fresh, without any body odor or other indication that it had been worn and not laundered thereafter. I made up my mind to argue in summation that the shirt had been cleaned to remove bloodstains or other incriminating material.

There was nothing in the father's direct testimony that threatened to stir the sympathy of jurors, and I was heartened when, upon cross-examination, William Mitchell actually transformed himself into a prosecution witness.

"Incidentally," I asked him, "you've also had conversations with your son with respect to his whereabouts on the morning of July 20, 1963, have you not?"

"Yes, I did."

"And, as a matter of fact, with respect to your son's whereabouts and what he did that night, you know for a fact that he lied to you?"

Lyon jumped out of his seat, yelling, "That is objected to, Your Honor!"

"Overruled," Judge Thompson said.

"Yes, he did originally," William went on.

"He lied more than once, didn't he, sir?"

"He lied to the fact that he said he came home at one o'clock."

"If Your Honor please, I think that calls for a yes or no answer," I said.

"Repeat the question," Judge Thompson said to the court reporter.

"He lied more than once, didn't he, sir?"

William Mitchell hesitated. "Answer the question," directed the judge.

"Yes, he did."

"The first time he told you he got home at one o'clock, is that correct?" I continued.

"That's correct."

"And then he told you he got home later than one o'clock, is that true?"

"That's correct."

"And you don't know what time he got home, do you, sir?"

"I didn't look at the clock. I don't know exactly what time he got home. I testified to that."

The defense certainly would have been better off had William Mitchell not testified. Actually, there was only one defense claim to which the father's testimony could be relevant and that was the contention that the defendant had been physically threatened and coerced into confessing by the police. William Mitchell failed to support this contention credibly. It was becoming clearer that the only substantial argument for reasonable doubt that Lyon would have to rely on was Winston Moseley's confession. During my summation, I would absolutely have to convince each and every juror, regular and alternate, that all of the credible evidence pointed to Alvin Mitchell's guilt. This might be the only way to prevent

Lyon from getting that one juror to hold out for acquittal.

William Mitchell's testimony consumed the entire morning, but the afternoon session was unexpectedly brief. A meteorologist took the stand to establish that the defendant had arrived home in the early morning hours of July 20—he knew this, because he had been told by members of Mitchell's family that it was still quite dark outside when Mitchell arrived home. The witness used weather reports from the vicinity of LaGuardia Airport, the weather station closest to the Mitchell residence. Unfortunately for the defense, the witness couldn't pinpoint the time the defendant arrived home based on lighting conditions outside.

Mary Mitchell, the defendant's mother, followed the meteorologist. Her appearance was an attempt to substantiate her husband's testimony that the infamous black T-shirt worn by Mitchell on the night of July 19 had been removed by police detectives from a pile of dirty laundry in the Mitchell's living room. The T-shirt had obviously been cleaned, but Lyon again wanted the mother's testimony to contradict any inference that it had been washed by the Mitchell family. There was no testimony from Mrs. Mitchell during direct examination to support the defense claim of a forced confession, and my cross-examination of her was brief. It was my intention during summation to express some sympathy toward the defendant's family, thereby making them a non factor in the jury's deliberations.

As Mary Mitchell left the courtroom, Judge Thompson recessed the trial until the following morning. No sooner had the jury filed out than Lyon asked Judge Thompson to release to the defense the taped interview in which Moseley allegedly described how he had killed Barbara Kralik. This tape recording, made by the killer's attorney Sidney Sparrow, had been a court exhibit in the first trial, though Judge Shapiro hadn't allowed it into evidence. As in the first trial, I vigorously opposed Lyon's request.

Despite the previous ruling by Judge Shapiro, after listening to arguments from Lyon and me and to statements from two of Moseley's court-appointed attorneys, Judge Thompson decided to hold a hearing to determine whether it was legally proper for either counsel to hear the tape. It would be held the following day, without the jury.

I went to see Frank O'Connor. The Chief, a perceptive person who remembered our last discussion about the tape recording, interrupted me when I brought it up. "Charlie," he said, "I recall how upset you were when you found out that we hadn't disclosed its existence to you, but in the end, your case wasn't hurt by your not knowing about it. It wasn't used in evidence in the first trial, and most likely it won't be used in this trial."

"That's not the point," I argued. "Undoubtedly, the tape contains a number of discrepancies between Moseley's description of the Kralik attack and the actual one. You actually told the media that there were such discrepancies. If I had heard the tape it would have helped me better prepare to cross-examine Moseley."

"Listen, Charlie, the tape was an interview of Moseley by his attorney. It wasn't intended to assist our investigation. Sparrow's purpose was to support Moseley's defense of insanity. Patten and I weren't present during the taping; we weren't permitted to question Moseley about the attack. I can't see how the tape can be any more helpful to you than Moseley's actual testimony in the first Mitchell trial, which did present some discrepancies."

The hearing, which consumed the entire day of March 2, proved to be much ado about nothing. After testimony from Bernard Patten and Moseley's three court-appointed attorneys, Judge Thompson ruled that the taped interview was hearsay and a privileged communication between Moseley and his counsel and couldn't be listened to by the defense, the prosecution, or the jury. In effect, it echoed Judge Shapiro's ruling.

The next day, before the jury was brought out, I announced in open court that William Finn was in the building, having been produced by court order, and was available if the defense wished to call him as a witness. Of course, I had no objection to Lyon speaking to Finn before calling him as a witness. Lyon cast me a contemptuous look without responding. I could sense that he was afraid of something. Judge Thompson had no comment.

Lyon's next witness was Arthur Mandella, a New York City detective assigned to the Bureau of Criminal Identification. He testified that none of the fingerprints or palm prints found at the Kralik crime scene matched either Moseley's or Mitchell's. Although Mandella added that several fingerprints and palm prints had never been identified, on cross-examination he said it wasn't unusual to find such prints at a crime scene.

When Mandella stepped down, Judge Thompson directed Lyon to call his next witness.

"Winston Moseley," the defense counsel announced in a resounding voice.

At once a murmur rose, and the assembled crowd began craning their necks and scanning the room, not knowing that there was only one door the killer could enter from, on the left side of the courtroom leading from the detention cells. Anticipation hung in the air, thickening as the few minutes ticked by and Moseley didn't show. It turned out that he was still in a receiving pen on the first floor, where he'd been delivered from Sing Sing, the state prison at Ossining. While the court waited, Judge Thompson directed Lyon to call an interim witness, Detective John Palmer.

I could almost feel the disappointment in the courtroom as Palmer approached the stand. Primed to view an infamous butcher in the flesh, the spectators must have hoped that this witness would be questioned quickly. And he was. Lyon attempted to establish that Palmer had obtained a detailed description of Barbara's assailant from a member of the Kralik family. This, of course, had never happened. The questioning fizzled out, and Palmer was excused.

CHAPTER EIGHTEEN

Herbert Lyon called out Moseley's name once again, and again the murmur appeared, only to be cut short by deafening silence when he finally made his debut.

Winston Moseley had put on weight, and his permanent icy stare, once unfathomable, now struck me as the demeanor of a vicious predator. Though all eyes in the courtroom were fixed on him, he displayed no emotion. It was as if he didn't have the slightest interest in what was going on around him. As he was being sworn in, out of the corner of my eye I could see all the reporters and spectators eagerly soaking up the sight. No one was going to miss a single word or gesture while Winston Moseley was in the courtroom.

I turned to Jack Peters and whispered, "This could be the whole ball of wax. If I can just get him once to blurt out that he didn't kill Barbara." Any testimony in which he described killing Barbara, regardless of how it might contradict the known facts, could win Lyon the one juror he needed to prevent a conviction

Judge Thompson directed Martha Zelman, the only one of Moseley's three court-appointed attorneys in the room, to stand beside him during his testimony and provide any legal advice he might need.

Lyon approached the podium that we used during the trial for the examination of witnesses. Some of the confidence seemed to have

189

drained out of him. He turned to look back at his associate, Bill Santoro as if to say, "Here goes." I almost looked at Lyon's fingers to see if they were crossed for good luck.

"Mr. Moseley," Lyon asked, "can you tell us where you were on the early morning of July 20, 1963?"

Moseley leaned toward his lawyer for a whispered consultation. Then he sat back and, staring directly at Lyon, said in a clear, determined, and hostile voice, "I refuse to answer any questions on this case."

Instantly, Lyon turned and addressed Judge Thompson. "If Your Honor please, I will ask whether the District Attorney will offer Winston Moseley immunity from prosecution for the murder of Barbara Kralik or for any perjury that he may be charged with as a result of previous testimony."

I stood up and announced, "I reassert at this time that the District Attorney of Queens County will not at any time prosecute Winston Moseley for the killing of Barbara Kralik or for any perjury committed in connection with his testimony as to the killing of Barbara Kralik."

Lyon turned to Moseley. "Tell us where you were on the early morning of July 20, 1963."

Like spectators following a tennis ball sailing over the net, every head in the room turned from Lyon to Moseley, transfixed. The jurors were alert as ever, straining to hear Moseley's response, and so was everyone else, Judge Thompson included.

In one fell swoop, Winston Moseley declared what I had believed all along was the absolute truth and what I had sweated blood to try and convince others of.

"The only further thing I have to say," he declared without skipping a beat, "is that I didn't do it, and I don't intend to go into any explanation."

If only he had said this from the beginning, my life and many others' would have been a lot easier!

Without hesitation and without giving himself time to absorb what he had just heard—Lyon asked, "You say now you didn't kill Barbara Kralik, is that correct?"

"That's right."

Winston Moseley was no longer a witness for the defense.

The words seemed to strike a blow at Lyon. He stumbled back, and for a moment I thought he was going to keel over. Jack Peters and I looked at each other without uttering a word. This was exactly what we were hoping for. It wasn't a scenario we could have written, let alone imagined.

Almost instinctively, I gave in to a temptation that I'd resisted up to this point—I turned around and glared at the reporters who over the past year had delivered such a terrible beating to the DA's office. They were feverishly scribbling away in their steno pads. Edye Cahill of the *World-Telegram*, who had been doing investigative legwork for the defense and whose hostile articles had betrayed her partisanship, appeared on the verge of an emotional breakdown. My gaze zeroed in on her. "Next time keep an open mind," I said silently with my lips.

Moseley had a habit of wreaking havoc. He'd killed with abandon, he'd made life hell for the DA's office and me, and now he was making these reporters eat crow.

"Go outside, and call Frank O'Connor," I whispered to Jack. "He needs to know right away. I'm sure some reporter will call him for a statement before the end of the day."

Moseley refused to answer any more questions from Lyon, other than to say that he didn't remember. Repeatedly, Judge Thompson held him in contempt of court, but it was a meaningless threat for a person already under a sentence of death.

Finally, with my consent, Judge Thompson permitted Lyon to read to the jury all of Moseley's testimony from the first Mitchell trial.

It consisted of almost forty pages of text. Lyon omitted several questions and answers that he obviously believed to be harmful to his client's interests. A mistake, I thought, as I intended to read them when Lyon had completed his direct examination.

In the first Mitchell trial, Moseley had testified to details of the killing of Barbara Kralik, but the testimony read by Lyon didn't have the same impact as that oral testimony would have had. I could see it in the jurors' eyes, which were glazed over.

When Lyon finished reading, he tried again to question Moseley, but it was no use, the man's lips were sealed shut. And so Moseley was turned over to me for cross-examination.

I rose. "I have no questions of this witness," I said loud and clear, denying Moseley the opportunity to recant.

Instead of cross-examining Moseley, I read the few questions and answers from his prior testimony omitted by Lyon. These included a statement to a doctor at Kings County Hospital during a psychiatric examination in which he denied killing Barbara Kralik.

As Moseley left the witness chair to head back to Sing Sing to await the outcome of his appeal from his conviction and death sentence, all the media people dashed out of the courtroom to phone in their stories.

Moseley's testimony seemed to have exhausted everyone in the courtroom except for Judge Thompson, who had Lyon call three more witnesses. Three police detectives, who had been present when Moseley was questioned on the night of his arrest, all testified to hearing him confess to killing Kitty Genovese, Annie Mae Johnson, and a girl in Springfield Gardens in 1963. Each said that no questions about the Kralik killing were asked that night. At the conclusion of their testimony, Judge Thompson recessed the trial until the following morning.

Leaving the courtroom, I was bombarded with questions from reporters, but I waved them off in my hurry to confer with Frank O'Connor, who wanted me to report to him straightaway.

With a smile on his face, he grabbed my hand and shook it, an uncharacteristic gesture. Before I even had a chance to sit down, the Chief said, "Tell me what Moseley said, verbatim if you can."

When I was done, O'Connor asked me if I thought the jury would believe him. "I think it got through to the jury," I responded. "There's no doubt that the reading of his prior testimony containing his purported confession wasn't nearly as effective as his denial in court today. In summation, I'll point out to the jury that we've been open about his confession, that we weren't trying to hide it from them but wanted them to see its flaws. It's important that I do this, because I objected to Moseley's tape recording going into evidence, and I prevented that statement of Barbara's about it being dark from going into evidence. Of course, it's still possible for the jury to think of Moseley as a serial killer, which could automatically connect him to the Kralik killing no matter what the proof to the contrary is." I couldn't resist asking O'Connor, "With this denial by Moseley, will you change your mind about a retrial of Mitchell in the event of a hung jury?"

"There won't be a third trial," the Chief said emphatically. Those words would continue to haunt me throughout the rest of the trial.

The following morning, Lyon attempted to attack the police for failing to investigate Moseley's connection to the Kralik homicide after his confession on the night of his arrest, but the ploy didn't work.

When the trial resumed in the afternoon, Lyon called Detective Joseph Fullam as a witness. I objected, knowing this would be a last-ditch effort to get into evidence the final words Barbara had uttered as the ambulance rushed her to the hospital. Judge Thompson ordered the jury to leave the courtroom and held a brief hearing after which he denied Lyon the opportunity to question Fullam.

"Call your next witness, please," Thompson directed Lyon.

"Alvin Mitchell," Lyon called out, looking at his client as he rose and started toward the witness chair.

As he passed the jury box on his way to the witness chair, Mitchell gazed directly at the faces of the people who would be judging him. He had been well coached. With his youthful good looks, wavy blonde hair, tailored blue suit and tie, he certainly didn't look like a person capable of stabbing a fifteen-year-old girl to death.

I didn't intend to spend much time punching holes in his description of the police interrogations. Instead, I believed, Mitchell's good looks and serene air could be overcome by damaging character evidence, and that's what I was going to concentrate on, his violent nature and criminal background. I also hoped to get something out of Mitchell to support the testimony of James Lewis, the bus driver.

Of course, if I were really lucky, Alvin Mitchell would break on the witness stand and blurt out the fact that he'd killed Barbara. But this wasn't a movie or television program. He had proven to be cunning, a well prepared witness at the first trial, repeatedly denying the murder even when his denials were not responsive to my questions. What hope I had of showing Mitchell to be a liar on the witness stand rested on this fact: a lie has to be remembered, while the truth isn't easily erased from the mind. Sir Walter Scott knew this well: "Oh, what a tangled web we weave when first we practice to deceive." Perhaps—but it was unlikely—the truth would slip out on the witness stand.

During the direct examination, Mitchell's statements were similar to those he'd given in the first trial, except that he painted a picture of more severe police brutality. He identified, by name, each of the officers he claimed had struck or otherwise abused him, including Inspector Fred Lussen and Detectives Charles Prasse and John Palmer. He even accused the stenographer from the DA's detective squad.

His next accusation set my blood boiling, and I made a note to confront him about it during the cross.

"Now, did there come a time when you told anybody that you'd tell them what they wanted to hear?" Lyon asked Mitchell.

"Yes, the 29th, the early part of the 29th. I told Detective McGuire. He took me into a room."

"Yes?"

"And he says, you ain't leaving this room alive unless you tell me that you killed Barbara Kralik. So I said, 'I'll sign anything.'"

"Wait a minute—how long had you been questioned before this happened?"

"About eight hours, maybe more."

McGuire was a convenient target of Mitchell's accusation. He had died before the first trial and was unable to refute the accusation.

Lyon's examination of his client was unexpectedly brief. It ended with a series of questions designed to convince the jury of his innocence. After each question, Mitchell would turn his head from Lyon and make eye contact with the jurors.

"Alvin, did you climb in the Kralik house on the morning of July 20, 1963?"

"No, I didn't."

"Did you stab Barbara Kralik?"

"No, I didn't."

"Did you ever stab Barbara Kralik?"

"No, I couldn't do something like that."

Next, Lyon had Mitchell fix his present height at five foot ten inches. Lyon was obviously going to argue in summation that the bus driver James Lewis slipped up by describing him as being only 5 foot 8. I didn't consider this a serious discrepancy. Frankly, the difference of only two inches after the passage of more than eighteen months in a hunched over youth was more helpful to the prosecution than the defense.

Lyon had left the door wide open for me to conduct an extensive cross-examination. I intended to fire questions at Mitchell, depriving him of the time to mull them over. He would be forced to answer more truthfully, since it would take time for him to search his memory for rehearsed testimony.

When I started my cross, Lyon, of course, realized my intent and repeatedly objected, delaying the process with speeches to give his client the opportunity to plan his answers.

I probed Mitchell about lying to his friends and telling them a neighbor had given him a ride home. "You lied to your friends, right?" I said.

"I told them that so they wouldn't argue with me."

"I didn't ask you that. Did you lie to your friends?"

"Yes, I did."

"And when you lied to your friends—"

Before I had a chance to complete my question, Lyon catapulted out of his seat one more time, "Now wait a minute, Your Honor. That is objected to. I ask that that be stricken…And I respectfully submit that the District Attorney is putting words in his mouth."

Judge Thompson quickly responded, "Overruled, this is cross-examination."

Lyon's constant interruptions were frustrating and fanned the growing hostility between prosecution and defense that had been building up throughout the trial. I complained to Thompson about the speechmaking, and the judge did try to restrain Lyon, telling him that I was doing no more than he had done during his own cross-examination of prosecution witnesses. At one point, Thompson threatened to hold Lyon in contempt, but he wasn't as forceful as Judge Shapiro and was unable to restrain him.

Despite the interruptions, I stuck to my basic plan, which was to depict the defendant as a violent person, especially when under the influence of alcohol. Mitchell was known as the "Monster" to his friends, and although Judge Thompson didn't permit me to question him about the origin of this nickname, I was allowed to pursue the issue of the other crimes he had committed. I was able to force Mitchell to admit that he'd been involved in several school burglaries and committed several assaults, some when under the influence of alcohol and a few when he had not had anything to drink. I certainly hoped this would dent his choir boy appearance. Gradually zeroing in on one of my central points, I asked him how much he'd had to drink on the night of July 19: "Now, what type of liquor did you buy first?"

"Fleischman's."

"Where did you buy the Fleischman's?"

"In a liquor store."

"There is a specific reason why you were the one that made the purchase of the Fleischman's, isn't there?"

"Yes, because I was eighteen."

"You say you had a bottle of Fleischman's to drink, you also had a bottle of wine?"

"Yes."

"Or part of a bottle of wine, is that correct?"

"We had a bottle of wine, but I only drank part of it."

"You drank half of it?"

"Yes."

"And how much of the Fleischman's did you drink?"

"Half."

"And you drank the six-pack of beer?"

"I drank the six-pack of beer, yes."

Pursuing Mitchell on his testimony about the claimed threat by Detective McGuire, I asked, "You do know now that Detective McGuire is dead?"

"I learned that the last trial."

"But dead men can't defend themselves, can they, Mr. Mitchell?"

"No, they can't."

"You also claim that Detective McGuire was drunk too, don't you?"

"He was."

I had always been concerned about my inability to find a witness who could prove directly that Mitchell had known that Pat Farfone had planned to sleep at the Kralik house on the night of July 19. Pat denied telling Mitchell, and she didn't know who had told him. In an attempt to corroborate this admission in his confession, I hammered away at him, and for once, Lyon refrained from interrupting.

"You said...you decided to go see Pat, because you thought she was sleeping in Barbara's house, is that right?"

"Yes."

"So you told Mr. Pryor that you thought Pat would be there, and maybe she would come into the car with you, is that right?"

"Yes, that's what I said."

"What police officer told you to say that?"

"I don't think any of them did."

"That was you own idea?"

"Yes, that was."

Straight from the horse's mouth. Here at last was the proof I'd been seeking. This admission denied Lyon the ability to argue his client hadn't known about the sleepover.

Shortly after, under rapid, uninterrupted questioning about the issue of the bus stop, Mitchell made a serious blunder.

"So that when you said to Mr. Pryor that you took a bus at Springfield Boulevard, you are telling us that you made that up. Isn't that right?"

"Yes, I made up the bus stop."

Mitchell's testimony on this point substantiated the accuracy of the testimony of James Lewis that he picked up the defendant in the early morning hours at the intersection of Springfield Boulevard and North Conduit Avenue. After all, why would Mitchell have to make up a bus stop if it wasn't true? Mitchell always claimed in his testimony in both trials that he had been given a ride home from Flushing. There would have been no need for him to mention a bus stop to either the police or Pryor, who did not know about the existence of Lewis during their investigation.

In my last few questions before the lunch break, I set the stage for refuting Mitchell's claim that it had been dark when he arrived home. I asked Mitchell how light it had been outside when he arrived home in the early hours of July 20. Mitchell was adamant; he said that it was "still dark."

"Pitch Dark?"

"Pitch Dark."

"You would not at any time say it was not quite light, is that correct?"

"No, it wouldn't be true. It was pitch dark."

My first questions when we returned from lunch were designed to challenge his credibility and also prove that he arrived home much later than he had testified to on direct examination.

"This morning you told us that you never described the lighting conditions when you arrived home on the morning of July 20 or the early hours of July 20 as being not quite light. Do you recall that?"

"Yes, I do."

Handing Mitchell the related part of the transcript of the first trial brought a puzzled look to his face.

"Do you remember the last trial?"

"Yes, sir"

"Were you asked this question, and did you give this answer? What time did you tell them?"

"I told them it was pretty late, but it wasn't quite light yet. It was about—I told them about 3:30."

"Did you make that answer to that question?"

"Yes, I did."

Hearing this, Judge Thompson jumped in with the following.

"This is the question that your own attorney asked you in the courtroom?"

"Yes."

"In this courthouse on trial?"

"Yes. But—"

"Pardon me, and you gave the answer that the District Attorney read?"

"Yes, I gave it to him."

It was a telling point. It suggested that the defendant had arrived home closer to 5:30 a.m., after he had committed the crime, when it would have been "not quite light," as opposed to his testimony today that he arrived home when it was "pitch dark," before the crime had occurred.

Thanks to Lyon's interruptions, the afternoon session ended with Mitchell still on the witness stand, which turned out to be a blessing for the prosecution. This gave me the entire weekend to work on my cross-examination and compare Mitchell's testimony to this point in this trial to his previous testimony in both trials.

Jack and I received the court reporter's transcripts of Mitchell's direct and cross-examination early Saturday morning and began going over his various testimony with a fine-tooth comb, especially his different accounts of how he got home on July 20.

Curious to know how reporters had reacted to Moseley's bombshell on the witness stand, on Saturday and Sunday I skimmed most of the articles in local newspapers. Incredibly, Edye Cahill of the *World Telegram* repeated her previous claims that Barbara had denied knowing her assailant and that he was dark skinned. Most of the other papers had returned to more objective reporting, especially the *New York Times*, *Long Island Press*, and *Star-Journal*. This was encouraging; any of the unsequestered jurors who were tempted to break the rule and read news about the trial might be getting a less biased version of events.

On Monday morning, I arrived in court raring to go, and my cross-examination proceeded exactly as designed. I confronted Mitchell with every different story he had told the detectives, one on July 21 and others on August 6, 26, 27, and 28, probing for every detail about his first claim of being given a ride home by a neighbor delivering a package to a movie theater, then by Finn, the make of the car, its color, and the route to Astoria.

"So you made up the Rambler?" I asked.

"I made up the make and the color, yes."

"And they told you they'd checked out every one of your stories."

"I only told them one, except for the color of the car and the blackout."

"Well, those are different stories, aren't they? The color of the car and the blackout, aren't they different stories?"

"The color of the car is the same story. The blackout is the only different story."

"And the police had a different story about a neighbor, is that right? Not from you, you said?"

"Not from me, that's right."

"But they told you they even checked out whether any neighbor of yours might have given you a lift, isn't that true?"

"Yes, they checked it out."

"And they said, everything you told us, we can't verify. Isn't that right? We can't find out anything that fits. Isn't that what they told you?"

"That's what they told me."

"And they told you, 'Mitchell, if you tell us the truth, we can eliminate you, and we won't bother you any more.' Isn't that what they said?"

"Yes."

"You told us before the luncheon recess that you never told the police that you were picked up in this ride that you claim you got by a neighbor, isn't that correct?"

"Yes."

Referring to Mitchell's prior testimony, I asked him, "Do you recall being asked these questions and giving these answers? But you told all your friends that you got a ride home by a neighbor, is that correct?"

"Yes. I did."

Lyon eventually jumped up, clearly agitated by the substance and manner of my questioning as well as the effect his client's answers were having on the jury. Angrily, he accused me of "playing games with this boy."

"No one's playing games with a boy in this trial," I snapped, annoyed by this accusation.

In one area, the defendant stood his ground. When it came time to review the statements he'd made to John Palmer, Stanley Pryor, and Jim Burnes describing the killing, he claimed it was all lies.

"I want to know if the police told you to say everything that you said in the statements to Pryor, to Palmer, to Mr. Burnes when he interviewed you outside police headquarters," I said.

"They didn't tell me everything to say," Mitchell replied, "but I knew everything by the questions they asked me."

Picking up the scissors that Dr. Grimes had testified to as being capable of producing Barbara Kralik's wounds, I asked Mitchell, "And they never tried to get you to say these are the scissors you stabbed her with?"

"No, they never did."

With this statement about the scissors still lingering in the air, I turned to the question of how Mitchell had reached home on July 20. I wanted to connect him to getting on Lewis's bus. I knew the questions I was about to ask were a long shot, but I had nothing to lose, because I had some corroboration already.

"Did you ever hitch a ride from Springfield Gardens to Astoria?" I asked Mitchell.

"I don't believe so," he replied.

"Did you ever try?"

"I tried."

"From where did you try to hitch?" I asked.

Without realizing the importance of this line of questioning, he answered, "On the Belt Parkway."

"And the service road of the Belt Parkway...is North Conduit Boulevard, isn't that right?"

"Yes."

The intersection of North Conduit Boulevard and Springfield Boulevard was the exact location where James Lewis had testified Mitchell boarded his bus. If there was a loose end in the prosecution case, it now seemed to be tied. In my summation I could recreate Mitchell's actions following his attack on Barbara: Borges had dropped him off on Springfield Boulevard, whereupon he walked a couple of blocks to North Conduit in the hope of hitching a ride. Unable to get a lift, Mitchell hopped on Lewis's bus when it arrived, took it to the Jamaica subway station, and from there caught a train to Astoria.

Mitchell appeared to be unnerved during the cross-examination. He was looking at the jurors less frequently than before; in fact, he was barely even looking in their direction. During my examination of Mitchell, I was as close to the jurors as I could get without sitting in their laps, and I could clearly see their reaction. Some were unable to look at Mitchell, an ominous sign for him, encouraging for me.

Having pulled more than I expected from Mitchell, I turned the battered defendant over to Lyon for the redirect. In a matter of minutes, Mitchell's testimony ended, he left the witness chair, and he shuffled back to his seat at the defense table, eyes on the ground. Lyon, having failed to restore his client's credibility on redirect, had to resort to stale tactics that hadn't worked to his advantage earlier. Repeatedly, he attempted to open the door to the statement that Barbara had allegedly made before dying, and every time he did, I jumped up and objected. Judge Thompson threatened to hold him in contempt if he continued pursuing this avenue. I could only hope the jurors wouldn't draw any unfavorable inferences from my objections to any references to the victim's alleged statement.

In a last-ditch effort to support Mitchell's testimony that it was dark when he arrived home, Lyon called MaryAnn Mitchell, the defendant's seventeen-year-old sister, to the stand and asked, "Now, do you know, was it light or dark when Alvin came home that night, if you know?"

"It was very dark when he came home," she quickly answered.

My cross-examination of Mitchell's young sister was brief and to the point. "Did you testify at the first trial, Miss Mitchell?"

"No, I did not."

"This is the first time you are saying this; isn't that correct?"

"That's right"

The statement could have muddied the waters, had MaryAnn come forward during the first trial or told Lyon about this earlier instead of waiting until two weeks before the second trial. As it was, she came off as a relative trying to help her brother. Her testimony struck me as artificial. As she was leaving the witness stand, I made a note to lump her testimony together with that of her mother and father and ask the jury to disregard all of it, because they were family members.

Realizing that Lyon was about to close the defendant's case, this was my last chance in the presence of the jury to get in a statement about his failure to call William Finn as a witness for the defense. I jumped up.

"Before counsel rests," I said, addressing Judge Thompson, "there is a court order, which made available one William Finn as a witness. He is presently in the building. This is the same William Finn that testified at the prior trial. I ask that the record indicate that Mr. Finn is available to be called as a witness if Mr. Lyon desires to call him."

As soon as I finished this remark, Lyon jumped up and argued, "[Mr. Skoller] already stated that outside the presence of the jury, but he didn't state that Mr. Finn, in the custody of the police department for traffic tickets, is brought here by him practically in chains as my witness. Now if he wants to run my case, he doesn't have to run it. I can get my own witnesses. They don't have to bring them in chains."

I was annoyed by my opponent's melodrama. "He was produced by court order by the District Attorney after Mr. Lyon requested it be done," I said, "and I intend to comment upon Mr. Lyon's failure to call him as a witness."

Obviously agreeing, Judge Thompson replied, "Then you may do it at the proper time."

Lyon moved for a mistrial, but his application was denied. Then the defense counsel closed his defense case without calling Finn as a witness.

To rebut certain inferences raised by Lyon during his questioning of Mitchell, I re-called Detectives John Palmer and Charles Prasse as witnesses. Through Palmer, I was able to get into evidence the hand-written statement he had taken from Borges on August 28, which closely paralleled the statement he'd taken from Mitchell. The details in the two accounts about what happened on the night of July19 through the morning of July 20 meshed, and now that both statements had been entered into evidence, the jurors could compare them during deliberations.

My next witness was Bernard Patten. He testified that no promises of a light sentence had been made to George Borges in exchange for his testimony. Patten did admit promising to report Borges's cooperation to the judge at the time of his sentencing for the school burglary. Lyon didn't cross-examine Patten, and Judge Thompson called a recess.

The following morning when Judge Thompson entered the courtroom, it was plain to see he was boiling. Without delay, he went into a tirade about certain articles in the press containing details of an alleged description by Barbara of her assailant that didn't fit any description of Alvin Mitchell.

"Mr. Lyon, I have noticed, and I am calling this to your attention, and I would like to make inquiry of you. In the past two days I have noticed in the public press a comment with respect to an ancient doctrine, dying declarations, and it appears that last evening in one of the papers a certain matter, which is not evidentiary, because it is not in evidence, was there alliterated and portrayed. I am not accusing you, sir, of a breach of faith with the court, but I gave you the right to look at certain documents for the purposes of identification, and I do not know for the life of me how the contents thereof could have been disclosed to the press except by the action of counsel, either on your part or the District Attorney's part or the witnesses themselves."

Lyon denied making any statements to the media. Although I could have informed on him—after all, I'd seen the defense attorney speaking to reporters on many occasions while the trial was in progress, especially the past few days—I held my tongue.

This trial day was consumed by yet another effort on the part of Lyon to get Barbara Kralik's last words into evidence. It was a brash stroke, especially in light of Judge Thompson's warning, for Lyon's speechmaking struck me as designed to impress reporters as much as the jurors. It was a long shot. There was nothing fresh about these rehashed arguments, and as Lyon droned on—Judge Thompson seemed unable or unwilling to stop him—they grew even staler. Finally, in exasperation, the judge directed Lyon to stop and ruled for the last time that no statements by Barbara Kralik would be received in evidence, because to do so would violate the rule of dying declarations.

That matter put to rest, I called the final witnesses in the trial: John Steinman and Henry Sardo, fellow employees of Mitchell who had testified in the previous trial. This time around, they repeated the same testimony that they'd worked with the defendant in August 1963 and seen him frequently during the workday. At no time did they observe Alvin Mitchell with the black eye his mother had testified to, and although the defendant had complained about being questioned by police officers, they never heard him say he'd been struck.

That brought the testimony to an end. Lyon promptly made a motion for the court to dismiss the case, and Judge Thompson, just as promptly, denied it.

Addressing Judge Thompson, Lyon made what many would consider an unusual and risky request.

"I also ask Your Honor at this time that the case be given to the jury as a murder one, or acquittal." Lyon's request was transparent. Considering Mitchell's age, and all the drinking he and Borges had done on the night of July 19, a conviction for murder in the first degree was improbable. Lyon must have anticipated that I would not pursue it.

Judge Thompson denied Lyon's request, informing him that he was going to submit to the jury the crimes of murder in the first degree and its derivatives: murder in the second degree, manslaughter in the first degree, and manslaughter in the second degree.

Whatever Judge Thompson decided regarding this matter, we wouldn't find out until he actually gave his instructions to the jury. The judge recessed the trial until the following day and asked counsel into his robing room.

"I want both summations to be completed in one day. I do not want any further delays in this trial. You, Mr. Lyon, will complete your summation in the morning and you, Mr. Skoller, will complete yours in the afternoon. There will be no extensions."

Jack Peters and I had already carefully prepared my closing argument, and I felt that the old college method of cramming would be counterproductive. Instead, what I needed was to relax. It was early afternoon when Jack drove me home, and I spent the rest of the day playing with my children. I went to bed early and, much to my surprise, had a good night's sleep. I woke up ready for the final act in what had proven to be an almost year-long ordeal.

CHAPTER NINETEEN

For many spectators, closing arguments are the highlights of criminal trials. This was quite apparent in the Mitchell case when Jack and I arrived on the morning of March 10 outside Judge Thompson's courtroom and had to push our gurney through the hallway full of boisterous, clamoring bodies. "Please, let us through!" We were practically begging them. The security situation still hadn't been addressed. As we inched forward, I was worried that someone would jostle our carefully arranged files, scattering them all over the place. When at last we reached the courtroom and were let in, I leaned against the doors in relief.

"I've never seen it so jammed," one of the court officers told me. It was true. Not even Moseley's trial had lured so many out of the woodwork.

Lyon and his associates were already seated at the defense table with their files and papers laid out in systematic order. The media representatives, who had come out in full force, occupied the first three rows of seats. Shortly after Jack and I finished sorting our files, the courtroom doors were unlocked, and the room filled with the sound of trampling feet.

At 10:00 a.m. on the dot, Judge Thompson entered the courtroom, followed shortly by the jury.

The court clerk announced, "No one will be permitted to leave during summation."

"All right, Mr. Lyon," Judge Thompson declared, "proceed with your summation."

Lyon must have had at least fifty yellow sheets with him as he approached the podium. He placed his notes on the podium, turned toward the jurors and, before saying a word, looked silently at each member. Then he expressed his appreciation to the jurors for their service and launched his argument. Unlike some lawyers, he didn't move about as he presented his summation. He remained motionless, lowering his head from time to time to glance at his notes and then returning to maintain eye contact with each juror. It was certainly effective, I thought.

"One fact I think that must be clear when you try to recall everything that happened is that in spite of some of the prodigious tasks and feats of memory that have been exhibited here, nobody is superhuman. We all make mistakes; we all forget testimony; we all find it difficult to recollect everything that happened, not only over a period of years but sometimes over a period of days."

It seemed obvious that Lyon had the bus driver in mind. Yet, surprisingly, instead of mentioning James Lewis, he referred to Stanley Pryor's testimony. This puzzled me. While Pryor's testimony was extensively detailed, it could hardly be described as a prodigious feat of memory.

"Regardless of the emotion I may show," Lyon went on, "regardless of any impression you may get as to how important it is to me personally for whatever reason I might have or sincerity or ambition or whatever it is to get Alvin Mitchell off, you are not going to decide the case on that. Regardless of whatever impression you may get from Mr. Skoller of how important it may be to him for whatever reason to get a conviction, you are not going to decide on that."

I made a mental note to respond to this in my summation. This trial wasn't a personal contest between attorneys; it was a search for the truth about who had killed a fifteen-year-old girl.

Lyon's summation took three hours, the entire morning, and as it unfolded, his modus operandi became apparent. He covered every area he contended established reasonable doubt requiring an acquittal, devoting roughly an hour to each. The first was the police investigation.

"Did you ever hear them say they never saw, never saw a policeman use force? Never? Some police department. Not that they are not conceding they use it for an arrest but never use force? Never lose your temper?"

He spoke of the various interrogations of Mitchell, concentrating on the long hours Mitchell had spent in the police station on six separate days and the intermittent nature of the questioning. In attempting to discredit the testimony of Stanley Pryor, Lyon drew attention to the time the assistant DA had stopped the Q&A to go to the bathroom, implying that he left so as to give the detectives a chance to "soften up" the suspect. In essence, Lyon was arguing that the interrogators were all lying, whereas the defendant was telling the truth about the beatings that he claimed to have received.

Of course, it was incumbent on the defense attorney to explain why his client had told different stories about how he'd made it home in the early morning hours of July 20.

Lyon argued that there weren't any changes in Mitchell's stories to the detectives. They were merely efforts on the part of a young man under the influence of alcohol to piece together the events of that night.

At no time during this part of Lyon's argument did I raise objections. His closing wouldn't, I sensed, be well received by a jury made up of law-and-order types and that didn't have a single minority representative.

The second part of Lyon's summation dealt with Winston Moseley's confession to killing Barbara Kralik. He pounced on the statement made by Moseley at the time of his first interrogation on March 18, 1964, in which he admitted killing a girl in Springfield Gardens in 1963.

"Now, I told you at the beginning of the case we are not here to prosecute Winston Moseley. That is not our job. But is it significant? 'I killed a girl in Springfield Gardens.' Not another question was asked? Not another question. If he didn't mean Barbara Kralik, then for all we know there is still a girl laying there that nobody checked out. But they knew he meant Barbara Kralik."

Then Lyon went on to read passages from Moseley's testimony in the first Mitchell trial that seemed to buttress his argument. It was a stretch. The only part of the original testimony that could in any way be linked to what happened in the Kralik house was Moseley's description of the victim's moans, because Barbara's parents had testified to hearing only moaning, no screams.

The murder of Barbara Kralik, Lyon argued, was the most vicious crime in the history of Queens County. Repeatedly, he submitted that only the likes of a monster such as Winston Moseley could have murdered Barbara Kralik in cold blood—certainly not his client, who was nothing more than a "high school dropout" and "drunken boy."

Staring sharply at each juror, Lyon slowly asked, "If Moseley had confessed first, who would I be defending?"

There was one glaring omission in this part of Lyon's summation. It completely skipped over Moseley's most recent testimony claiming that he hadn't killed Barbara Kralik.

However, the jurors appeared to be reacting to Lyon's argument, leaning forward and listening intently. No one was fidgeting. Concerned that Lyon was getting to them, I made a note to emphasize in my summation that Alvin Mitchell, and only Alvin Mitchell, could have killed Barbara Kralik, not Winston Moseley.

The final part of Lyon's summation was devoted to George Borges, William Finn, and James Lewis. His attack on the testimony of George Borges was twofold. Why had the boy said that he'd heard Mitchell confess to the crime? First, Lyon claimed, Borges had been looking to get a break in his sentence for the school burglary. Second, the police had used physical force to coerce him into making such a statement.

Regarding William Finn, I had forced Lyon's hand by pointing out before the jury that the witness was in a holding cell, ready to testify. Now Lyon had to produce an explanation for not calling Finn to the stand. What the defense attorney concocted was a knotty legal explanation that clearly flew over the heads of the jurors.

"Mr. Skoller gets up here in the court and says, 'I have brought a witness for you.' I submit it is highly improper, and I submit that I have a right now to be concerned. Who asked? How do you know I have not been looking all over for this fellow? You bring him? Put him on, if you got him, he can be your witness."

I could see a puzzled look on the faces of some of the jurors. Even I had trouble digesting the argument. But I was pleased that Lyon referred to the failure to call Finn, because it opened the door for me to refer to the failure as well as rebut the defense explanation in my summation.

Lyon reserved some of his last remarks for the testimony of James Lewis. Careful not to impugn the truthfulness of such a credible and impartial witness, Lyon actually argued that I had manipulated the bus driver.

"There's an honest man, but what can you do when you come up against somebody who's skilled enough to know how memory works?... Alvin and fifteen other people. We don't have lineups any more? There aren't pictures? Alvin and fifteen other people. Pick him out. You can't have it both ways. If this memory is that good, and he sees the shoes and remembers the date, and he went home and thought and thought, and he thought honestly, as I am sure he did, if he really remembered he would see the cut, wouldn't he? There was no cut on this boy, because it was not Alvin."

When it was time to wind up, Lyon looked exhausted and aged. His voice dropped for the first time as he looked at each juror in an effort to display sincerity.

"If I am right, and it makes sense, I have done my job. His life, then, is in your hands. His future, his liberty, whatever it is, and I ask for his liberty not because I am asking for sympathy but the case calls for it. If you remember at the beginning of this trial…I told you it is a deception to say and feel that you can only have a harsh duty in a murder trial. You can have the very great, important, human, and satisfying duty of realizing that if there is no proof beyond a reasonable doubt the boy is innocent, and he goes home. Thank you."

As soon as Lyon sat down, Judge Thompson called a lunch recess and rapped his gavel. I hurried out of the courtroom, elbowing my way to the elevator, ignoring reporters yelling out questions at me, and eventually made it to the peaceful sanctuary of my office.

I spent the recess there, eating a sandwich that Jack had sent for, going over my cue cards and the notes I'd made during Lyon's summation. There are three summations in a trial: the one the attorney prepares, the one he delivers, and the one he would deliver if given a second chance. A closing argument is never cast in concrete. It's a work in progress—prepared, revised, and, even during the delivery, partly improvised and extemporaneous. Not even the lawyer delivering it knows exactly how it will turn out. I was aiming to make mine an hour and a half—half as long as Lyon's. After all, aren't brevity and clarity the soul of truth?

As I walked back to the courtroom, I could only hope that the words flowing from my mouth would spell out the truth of what had happened to Barbara Kralik on the night of July 19 and into the morning of July 20, 1963, and overcome the obstacle of Winston Moseley.

As soon as Jack and I began laying out cue cards and notes and exhibits in the order I intended to use them, the courtroom filled up again. Judge Thompson emerged from his chambers, followed shortly by the defendant and then the jurors. I made a mental note not to glance in the direction of the audience at any time. My concern was with the jurors only.

"Proceed, Mr. Skoller," Judge Thompson directed.

Stepping up to the podium in a charcoal gray suit with a conservative tie, I was as relaxed and focused as I could hope to be, despite some butterflies. Because of the positive changes in the evidence, I was more confident at the start of this summation than I had been in the first trial.

My opening remarks were designed to complement what I knew Judge Thompson would tell the jurors was their duty: to seek out the facts. "Select the facts you find to be true," I said. "This is your obligation when you go into that room, to try and find what the truth is, to try and find if there's any explanation for the death of a fifteen-year-old girl. That's our obligation here. And none of us take it lightly, whether we be young or old." With this I stared directly at Lyon, who was some fifteen years older than I.

I knew right from the start of my summation that the jurors were hanging on my every word. Unlike Lyon, I moved frequently from the podium to the prosecution table, some ten feet away. Except to glance quickly at my notes and to look for and pick up an exhibit in evidence, I tried to maintain my eye contact with the jurors.

Slowly, meticulously, taking care not to exaggerate any testimony, I reviewed the events of July 19 and 20.

"This trial," I emphasized, "started with Alvin Mitchell...started with a burglary of a school, where the defendant procured the weapon that took the life of Barbara Kralik and in the process of burglarizing the school a few things happen, a cut occurs on the wrist, the right wrist of Alvin Mitchell...and he wrapped the shirt around the wrist, exactly as described by Lewis. But what happened in the Kralik house? Marie Kralik nudges her husband and wakes him up, and they both go into the room, and they find their daughter mortally stabbed." I showed the jurors the photograph of Barbara's bed with the covers off to one side. I continued: "This is a photograph of the bed gentlemen. And Mrs. Kralik testified that when they entered that room these covers were as they appear. Those covers were on that bed." I emphasized this, because Mitchell's confession stated he thought he saw two people in the bed.

"What is the nature of the room?" I went on. "We know it's a small room. We also know the weather this night. We know, no question, no moon was out, no sun was out. It was nighttime, no stars were out. The only street light nearby was obscured by trees...That room was pitch dark, and nobody could see in that room beyond a shadow, possibly."

As I emphasized these details, I sensed that my words were getting through to most of the jurors, if not all. Several peered at the photograph, and I saw a few nod their heads as if in agreement with what I was saying.

Next, I addressed Mitchell's questioning—the different stories he told the police about how he got home, including the stranger, the neighbor, and the car described as a Rambler, though we knew Finn had a Ford Falcon. I then proceeded to discuss the statements in which both Mitchell and Borges told the detectives and Pryor that Mitchell was dropped off at a bus stop on Springfield Boulevard after his vicious attack on Barbara. Comparing Borges's statement to Mitchell's, I argued, "How could these statements be anything but factual? They so clearly corroborate each other."

Midway through my summation, as I had planned, I proceeded to take Lyon to task for not calling William Finn as a defense witness. "Certainly," I said, "the defense doesn't have to prove anything in a trial, but suppose you have the person who drove you home to Astoria before the crime occurred, and you don't call him as a witness. What can you infer from that?"

Lyon bounced out of his chair. "Objection!" he screamed.

"Overruled," Judge Thompson said.

"Thinking of William Finn, I'll take a break and look at an empty witness chair." I turned to stare at the chair as Lyon jumped up again.

"Objection!"

"Overruled."

Silently, I cast my gaze on the chair. Then I turned back to the people in whose hands Mitchell's fate rested and looked into each of their eyes, one after another. "Lyon said in his closing he didn't know where Finn was. I told him with you present that Finn was next door."

"Objection!"

"Overruled."

After a few moments, I picked up the container with the filmed confession that Alvin Mitchell had made to Jim Burnes.

"This may be the most significant item of evidence of all, because this cannot be distorted. This cannot be a lie. And this you have to analyze very, very carefully, gentlemen, more carefully than you can possibly imagine; this little tin container. And this tells a story that's quite incredible…[I'll] have this shown to you again and try and get as close to…the screen as you possibly can…Look at Mitchell's physical appearance in this after eight hours of being hit over the head with a folded-up newspaper…This film more than exhibits the defendant's physical appearance. You've got to listen to the sound. Oh, what an education. 'Did you think you'd get caught?'…And what's his answer? 'I wanted to tell them from the beginning, but I was scared'…The defendant himself admitted under cross-examination, 'Nobody told me to say it.' That indicates two things. Number one, this is his language. And number two, a consciousness of guilt. He knew it was all over. 'I wanted to tell them from the beginning, but I was scared.' He told the police because he was scared? No. He didn't tell the police because he was scared. And there's a big difference between the two. Take that film into your jury room. It can't possibly lie to you, gentlemen…It tells a story that's incredible, to say the least. 'Do you think you should be punished for it?' 'Yes.'"

Now it was time to tackle the issue of Winston Moseley. One by one, I broke down the details in his testimony in the first trial that had been read to the jurors. Moseley had said there were only three people in the Kralik house. Not true, there were five. He said the house was in the middle of the block. Not true, it was on a corner. He said nobody was sleeping in the first bedroom. Not true, that was where the grand-mother slept. He said the weather was warm, clear, and dry. Not true, it was rainy. He said he stabbed the girl with a serrated steak knife. Not true, the medical examiner said such a weapon couldn't have caused the wounds. And while Moseley consistently maintained that he killed Kitty Genovese and Annie Mae Johnson, he twice denied killing Bar-bara Kralik—once in this trial and once to psychiatrists at Kings County Hospital before his own trial.

By now I'd been speaking for about an hour, and it was time to start winding up. How had the crime occurred? Lyon had offered his version, full of tangled distortions, now it was time for me to put it in the per-spective that the evidence established.

"I want to go over the coincidences in this matter. I want to go into an explanation. How does a fifteen-year-old girl, who is defended by at least four members of her family—you have to pass four sleeping mem-bers of her family in order to get to her room—how does she get stabbed in her own bed?…There has to be some explanation. Nobody went into that house without being familiar with that house, without knowing the layout of the house. Moseley didn't even know there was a kitchen; there was a dining room and a living room when you came downstairs in order to go to the side door. When you come down those stairs in that house you are a few feet from the front door, you go right out the front door. That's where you should go, if you don't know the house. But if you know the house you have to use the side door, because the front door is stuck…But Moseley went directly from the stairs to the kitchen and out the side door. This is what he said. He could have learned a few things additional. He read about it in the newspaper. And he says, months after the girl was killed, he went near the house, passed by the house..."

"You've got to know that house. You had to have been in there. You had to know and...know the reason why you were going into the room, however illogical it is. There was a reason that's the room the person wanted to go...If you want to kill, go to the first door, the grandmother's door facing you as you come up the stairs. No, that person who went into that room had a reason in his mind for going into the room. And the person who went out the side door knew that the front door was stuck..."

"Senseless killing? Absolutely...Would he have done it if he wasn't a little drunk, if he didn't have liquor in him? I don't know. But with liquor in you, you get courage, you burglarize schools and...you think maybe Pat will be sleeping over this night, and you go into that room and Pat is not there, but you think she is, because you think you see two people sleeping in that bed..."

"Let's look at the coincidences. Coincidence, Mitchell was familiar with the house. Coincidence, he knew that when Pat slept over she slept in that room. Coincidence, he happened to have stolen scissors on the night in question...Coincidence, he is dressed in a black T-shirt and pants. Coincidence, he has sandy-colored hair. Coincidence, he cut his right hand and at some point or another he wrapped a handkerchief around it. Coincidence, he says, 'I went to the bus stop on Springfield Boulevard.' Coincidence, he is seen, a few minutes after the killing, boarding that bus on Springfield Boulevard, by a person who has absolutely no reason to perjure himself. Coincidence, and perhaps this is the biggest coincidence of all, when the bus made the turn at 140th Avenue and Farmer's Boulevard [one short block from the Kralik house], Mitchell's head was leaning out the window. What was he listening or looking for?"

At this moment, I stopped and quietly scanned the faces of the jurors. I raised my voice and called out, "Barbara Kralik is not dead by coincidence!"

Now was the time to end. I knew it would be counterproductive to prolong my argument. I uttered in a low, expressive voice, "I say to you with the utmost sincerity, I want you to believe that the People of the State of New York seek no vengeance in this trial. We seek no glory. We seek the truth. Let your verdict speak the truth. Thank you, gentlemen."

These words spoken, I returned to my chair and sat down, exhausted but exhilarated. I had accomplished what I had set out to do. Regardless of the result, I wouldn't have changed one word of my summation. My work was done.

Judge Thompson announced to the jurors that court would recess until tomorrow morning at 9:30, at which time he would give them instructions before starting deliberations.

As soon as the jurors filed out of the courtroom, Judge Thompson summoned Lyon and me to his robing room. "There's a problem with one of the jurors," he told us.

Not another problem, I thought, my heart sinking.

Apparently, one of the jurors had reported that another juror said he didn't give a damn how long the case went on, he had made up his mind a long time ago, and he wasn't going to change it.

"I'm going to question the juror briefly," Thompson said, wearily, "then decide what to do tomorrow morning before my charge to the jury."

I went home early to catch up on my rest. Several reporters called, including Richard Johnston of the *New York Times*. He was surprised that I hadn't asked the jury to find the defendant guilty, which is customary for a prosecutor at the end of a summation.

"I was looking for the truth in this trial, and that's what I asked of the jury," I told him off the record. "I just want the jurors to put the lie to Moseley's confession once and for all. After all, that's their responsibility, not mine and not the media's. Some of your colleagues seem to have forgotten this."

I spent the rest of the night trying to unwind and not second-guess the decisions I'd made during the trial. However, as I played with Beth, Robert, and Caren, as always, I couldn't help thinking of Barbara Kralik again. This thought, and the possibility that Mitchell might get away with it, continued to haunt me. Frank O'Connor wouldn't change his mind. Another hung jury and there wouldn't be another trial.

When Jack and I arrived at the courthouse the following morning, the crowd was spilling out of the building onto Queens Boulevard, boisterous as ever. There was always electricity in the air when a judge was about to charge a jury and the spectators were awaiting the verdict.

When I walked through the doors of the courtroom, it was filled to capacity, and several court buffs called out to wish me good luck. I nodded but made no answer.

At 9:30, Judge Thompson summoned Lyon and me to his robing room, then sent for the juror about whom the complaint had been made. After the judge put several questions to him, it was clear that the juror had indeed made up his mind and shouldn't be permitted to continue serving. With the consent of both Lyon and myself, the man was excused, and Judge Thompson directed that he be permanently removed from the juror rolls.

At last we returned to the courtroom, where an alternate juror was selected. Then Judge Thompson ordered the room locked and, without further ado, commenced his charge to the jury.

"Mr. Foreman and gentlemen of the jury," the Judge started, "at the outset I hasten to explain to you that your service as jurors is an active part of the administration of justice. It is a privilege, because it is part of our democratic system of government translated into action."

Thompson's instruction to the jurors turned out to be almost seventy-six pages long. For almost two hours, the judge read it, slowly and carefully, without any interruption except to raise his head and look at the jurors.

This being the first murder trial over which he'd presided, Thompson had obviously done his homework, researching and studiously preparing the charge. Unlike some judges, he thoroughly marshaled the evidence, that is, he summarized the testimony of each and every witness called to the stand. It was as impartial as it could be. Neither the prosecution nor the defense benefited from his presentation. Surely the summary was the product of copious notes taken during the trial, not just from the daily trial transcripts prepared by court reporters.

Thompson had previously denied Lyon's request that only the charge of murder in the first degree be submitted to the jury, and now he told the jury that they could consider the lesser degrees of criminal homicide: murder in the second degree, manslaughter in the first degree, and manslaughter in the second degree. He also instructed the jury to consider whether statements allegedly made by the defendant were voluntary and truthful, and to disregard them if it wasn't proved beyond a reasonable doubt that they were voluntary.

Thompson's instructions on reasonable doubt were textbook applications of the approach approved time and time again by the New York Court of Appeals. As the judge completed his charge, I couldn't help but compare it favorably to the one Shapiro had made in the first Mitchell trial, in which he had permitted his mistrust of police testimony to permeate his instructions to the jury. Judge Thompson didn't refer to Nazi Germany or Communist Russia.

Although I disagreed with some of the language Judge Thompson used, I didn't take issue with any part of the charge, nor did I make any additional requests to charge. Lyon made twenty additional requests, all directed to the judge's marshaling of the testimony. Some were accepted, and Judge Thompson instructed the jury accordingly.

That taken care of, it was time for the jury to do their work. At 11:50 a.m., they filed out of the courtroom to begin deliberations.

CHAPTER TWENTY

As always, when I was waiting for a jury verdict, I was restless. With the knowledge that I needed twelve jurors to decide a guilty verdict, I couldn't help feeling apprehensive.

My small office was packed with many of the assistant DAs in my bureau and most of the key detectives who had testified. Although it was noisy, I didn't seem to hear it. Joseph Kralik dropped by to speak to Captain Dowd and me. He'd been traveling back and forth between Marie Kralik in the hospital and the courthouse, and he looked haggard, concerned about the outcome of the case. The others left, and Joseph thanked us on behalf of himself and his wife, for "doing the best for my daughter."

"Anything could happen with a jury," I warned him. "The trial isn't over until a verdict is reached, and if there's another hung jury there won't be a third trial."

"I understand," he said and told me he was leaving for the hospital to stay with his wife. "Here's the phone number. Can you give me a call when the verdict's reached?"

"I promise."

As Dowd and I were about to leave for lunch, my old mentor Frank Cacciatore showed up. He and I hadn't spoken to each other about the Mitchell case since he'd been sworn in as a criminal court judge.

"How'd the trial go?" he asked, warmly patting me on the back.

221

"I'm not making any predictions," I replied, "but I think my case is much stronger than in the first trial."

"Charlie, I've been following the trial in the press, but I can't even guess from the one-sided accounts in the papers. The Moseley turn-around and the bus driver's testimony should alter the equation. It doesn't necessarily mean a guilty verdict, but it won't be eleven to one for acquittal. No matter what any newspaper prints, the office was justified in trying Mitchell a second time. No question about it."

I'd known that all along, but it was gratifying to hear the words from someone else, especially from one for whom I had a great deal of respect and affection. "The Chief told me in the event of a hung jury there won't be a third trial. What do you think, Frank?"

"He's right. A second hung jury will prove a verdict impossible. The office has to let go of the case and let the burglary charge stand in place of a homicide conviction."

After Cacciatore left, Dowd and I went to lunch at the Pastrami King near the courthouse. The crowd milling around outside made a path for us as we crossed the street. We didn't discuss the case during lunch. Instead, we talked about our children, and Dowd asked me about plans for the future.

"I'll stay in the DA's office as long as the Chief is there," I said. "I want to get as much trial experience as possible before leaving."

Dowd laughed. "I'd say the Mitchell case has given you a lifetime of professional experience."

"Isn't that the truth!" I answered.

I remained in my office the rest of the afternoon, trying to read over the files of some future trials, but I was too distracted to make much headway and ended up twiddling my thumbs. There wasn't a peep from Judge Thompson or the clerk. Apparently, the jury had ordered lunch and dinner brought in to the jury room.

I stepped out for dinner with Jack, and upon my return, I received a message from Judge Thompson saying that the jury would be returning to the courtroom at about 7:00 p.m. to hear some testimony read back: Joseph Kralik's entire testimony and certain portions of Borges's testimony. I felt as if I'd been punched in the stomach. These were two areas of testimony that Lyon had vigorously pressed in his summation and that had apparently stuck in the minds of some jurors. I was puzzled by these requests and concerned that perhaps the jurors didn't believe Borges and were trying to fit Joseph Kralik's testimony into a puzzle that favored the defense. Fortunately, the jury had also asked to have Mitchell's filmed confession replayed to them. That was a ray of hope.

Jack Peters and I made our way over to the courtroom to hear the court reporter read the requested portions of testimony. Judge Thompson removed everyone from the courtroom except me, Jack, Herbert Lyon and his associates, and Alvin Mitchell. The room was darkened, and the film played. Some jurors left the jury box and approached the screen, getting as close as possible without blocking the view of other jurors. The film was played one time, and the jury, satisfied, left to continue their deliberations.

Back in my office again, I tried to keep busy with the files of my other cases, but soon my eyes glazed over. Several reporters dropped by to ask for comments, but I refused to talk. The normal workday hubbub outside my office had long ago died down, and as the night wore on, I could hear the seconds ticking away sluggishly.

Midnight passed without another word from the jury. Their silence fanned my fear of another hung jury. The men had already been deliberating longer than their counterparts in the Shapiro trial. Was there some problem—some argument among the jurors?

At 1:00 a.m., I received word that another note had been received from the jury. With a sense of dread I rushed to the courtroom, which was, at this ungodly hour, still packed with reporters and spectators. My concern was short-lived. The jurors had requested that Judge Thompson redefine the different degrees of criminal homicide. I closed my eyes, resisting the temptation to shout with joy. This doesn't mean they'll convict, I told myself as the jurors filed back to the jury room, though I couldn't think of any other reason they would want the different definitions of homicide spelled out.

Judge Thompson repeated his instructions with respect to the different degrees of criminal homicide, and the jurors again left the courtroom to continue their deliberations.

Before I had a chance to return to my office, another note was received from the jury stating they had reached a verdict. Momentarily, Dowd and the other detectives appeared in the courtroom. As they were coming in, Mitchell's parents got up and departed, looking too shaken to hear the outcome.

At 1:35 a.m., the jury filed into the courtroom and took their seats. Each juror looked straight ahead, avoiding even a glance in the direction of the defense table.

"Have you agreed upon a verdict?" the clerk of the court asked.

With an air of confidence and what seemed like a sense of relief, the foreman of the jury stood up and answered. "Yes, we have."

"Jurors, please rise," the court clerk directed. "Look upon the defendant. Defendant, rise. Look upon the jurors." The clerk paused. "What's your verdict?"

The foreman quickly and clearly announced, "We, the jury, find the defendant guilty of manslaughter in the first degree."

Upon hearing these words, I leaned so far back in my chair that it almost tipped over. Jack Peters instantly put his arm around my shoulder to steady me and whispered "Congratulations." Immediately Dowd, Palmer, Prasse, and Stankus crowded around me, all as excited as I was. Although the outcome of my struggle had not yet fully sunk in, I felt personally vindicated for having pressed for the second trial and the opportunity to prove Mitchell's guilt. I was also proud I hadn't given up hope that a jury would search for and find the truth.

After thanking the jury on behalf of the People of the State of New York, I hurried out of the courtroom to phone Frank O'Connor and Joseph Kralik. Reporters pounced on me, asking for a reaction to the verdict. "I said all I needed to say during the trial," I answered them. What more could I add to the jury's verdict?

Then, utterly spent, I left the building and drove home. At the Chief's suggestion, I took the next week off to recuperate and make up for lost time with my children.

EPILOGUE

On Monday, March 14, 1965, I received a phone call from Bernard Patten, who asked me to meet with him and William Finn. At the meeting, Finn told us what I'd never doubted, that he hadn't given a ride to Mitchell and had never seen or met him before the first trial. His testimony in the first trial was untrue, and he had said so to Lyon at some point during the second trial. I wanted to charge Finn with perjury, but Patten and the Chief were opposed in view of his turnaround and refusal to commit perjury in the second trial. They didn't want to pursue the matter. I never found out the reason for Finn's sudden change of heart.

On May 6, 1965, Judge Thompson sentenced Alvin Louis Mitchell to a prison term of not less than ten and no more than twenty years, the maximum allowable for manslaughter in the first degree. A number of appeals and efforts to set aside his verdict and sentence failed.

After pleading guilty to attempted burglary in the third degree for his breaking and entering the school in Fresh Meadows on July 19, 1963, Mitchell was sentenced to an indeterminate prison term to run concurrently with his sentence on the manslaughter conviction. In other words, he didn't have to serve any additional prison time.

The death sentence Judge Shapiro imposed on Winston Moseley was reversed by the New York Court of Appeals. The high court decided that Judge Shapiro had committed reversible error during the sentence hearing by not permitting the jury to hear psychiatric testimony of Moseley's mental state as a mitigating circumstance. Returned to Judge Shapiro for another sentencing, Moseley received life in prison.

Several years into his term, Moseley escaped from custody while being transported to a hospital for medical treatment. While at large, he took an upstate New York family hostage and sexually assaulted the woman of the house. After a prolonged standoff, he surrendered to an agent of the FBI.

In 1999, Moseley brought on a petition in federal court to set aside his conviction on the ground that his attorney, Sidney Sparrow, had a conflict of interest. Apparently, at some point Sparrow had represented Kitty Genovese on a minor offense. Moseley's petition was denied, and as of this writing, the killer is confined to prison in upstate New York.

Winston Moseley was never brought to trial for the murder of Annie Mae Johnson. That indictment remains open in Queens County.

When Frank O'Connor assumed office as president of the New York City Council in January 1966, I left the DA's office to engage in private practice as a litigation attorney in civil and criminal matters.

During speaking engagements over the years, people have often asked me about the infamous Kitty Genovese murder. Why, they want to know, didn't someone call the police upon first hearing Kitty's screams? That question is best left to the psychologists and sociologists; I never did find an answer. One thing is certain, though: a human life is worth at least a telephone call.

Of course, it is worth a whole lot more than that, which is why I worked so hard to put the killers of Barbara Kralik, Kitty Genovese, and Annie Mae Johnson behind bars. Though these young women could not be given their lives back, at least justice was served on their behalf.